Defoe Abbott Marx Hardy Machiavelli Montaigne Chesterton Cooper Emerson Joyce Austen
Melville Haggard Hugo Grimm
Stoker Carroll Christie Molière Eliot
Wilde Byron Schiller
Garnett Maupassant Fitzgerald Engels Smith Kafka
Goethe Einstein Hawthorne Hall
Cotton Dostoyevsky Willis
Baum Henry Kipling Doyle
Leslie Dumas Flaubert Nietzsche
Stockton Turgenev Balzac
Burroughs Vatsyayana Crane
Curtis Tocqueville Verne
Homer Widger Tolstoy Gogol Vinci
Darwin Whitman Busch
Potter Freud Thoreau Twain Plato Scott
Kant Zola Lawrence Harte
Jowett Stevenson Dickens Hesse
Andersen Burton
London Descartes Cervantes
Poe Aristotle Wells Voltaire Cooke
Hale James Hastings
Bunner Shakespeare Irving
Richter Chambers
Doré da Shaw Benedict Alcott
Dante Chekhov Pushkin
Swift Wodehouse Newton

tredition®

tredition was established in 2006 by Sandra Latusseck and Soenke Schulz. Based in Hamburg, Germany, tredition offers publishing solutions to authors and publishing houses, combined with world-wide distribution of printed and digital book content. tredition is uniquely positioned to enable authors and publishing houses to create books on their own terms and without conventional manu-facturing risks.

For more information please visit: www.tredition.com

TREDITION CLASSICS

This book is part of the TREDITION CLASSICS series. The creators of this series are united by passion for literature and driven by the intention of making all public domain books available in printed format again - worldwide. Most TREDITION CLASSICS titles have been out of print and off the bookstore shelves for decades. At tredi-tion we believe that a great book never goes out of style and that its value is eternal. Several mostly non-profit literature projects pro-vide content to tredition. To support their good work, tredition donates a portion of the proceeds from each sold copy. As a reader of a TREDITION CLASSICS book, you support our mission to save many of the amazing works of world literature from oblivion. See all available books at www.tredition.com.

 Project Gutenberg

The content for this book has been graciously provided by Project Gutenberg. Project Gutenberg is a non-profit organization founded by Michael Hart in 1971 at the University of Illinois. The mission of Project Gutenberg is simple: To encourage the creation and distribu-tion of eBooks. Project Gutenberg is the first and largest collection of public domain eBooks.

Michelangelo A Collection Of Fifteen Pictures And A Portrait Of The Master, With Introduction And Interpretation

Estelle M. (Estelle May) Hurll

Imprint

This book is part of TREDITION CLASSICS

Author: Estelle M. (Estelle May) Hurll
Cover design: Buchgut, Berlin – Germany

Publisher: tredition GmbH, Hamburg - Germany
ISBN: 978-3-8424-8362-0

www.tredition.com
www.tredition.de

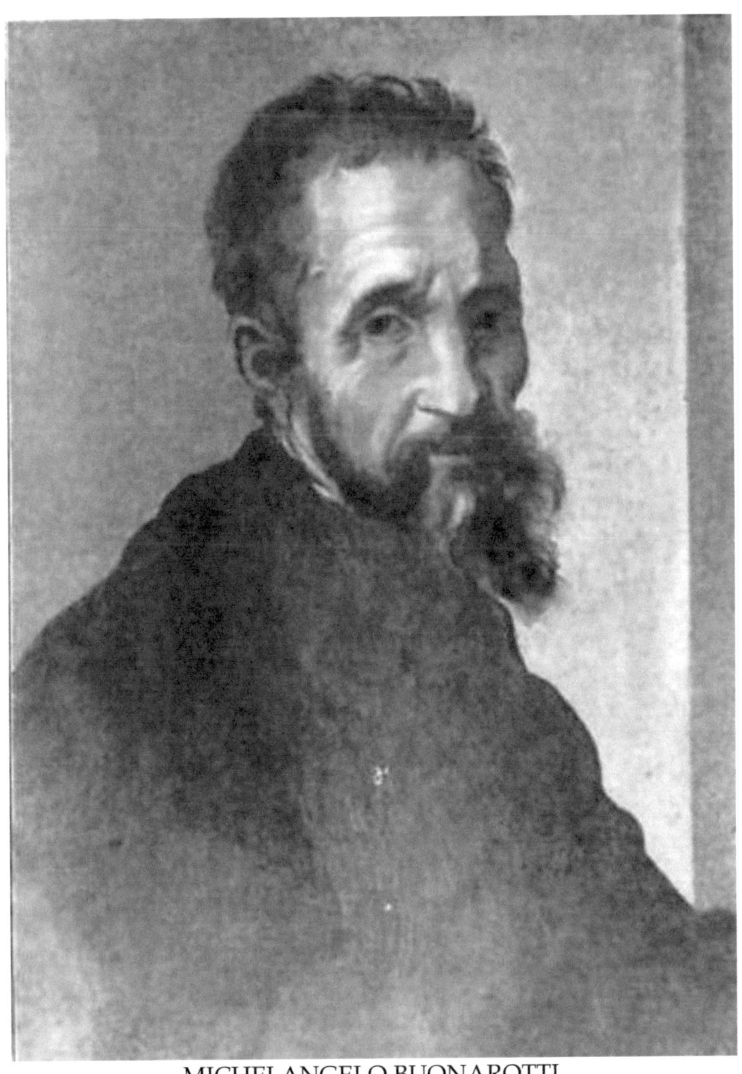

MICHELANGELO BUONAROTTI.
Attributed to Bugiardini. Uffizi Gallery, Florence.

The Riverside Art Series

MICHELANGELO

A COLLECTION OF FIFTEEN PICTURES AND A PORTRAIT OF THE MASTER WITH INTRODUCTION AND INTERPRETATION

BY

ESTELLE M. HURLL

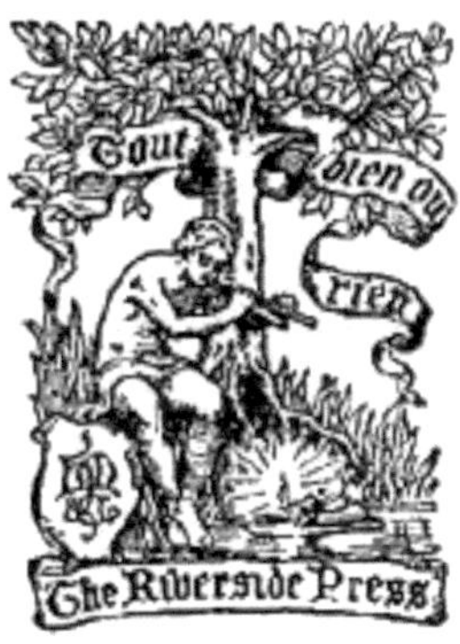

PREFACE

In making a collection of prints from the works of Michelangelo, it is impossible to secure any wide variety, either in subject or method of treatment. We are dealing here with a master whose import is always serious, and whose artistic individuality is strongly impressed on all his works, either in sculpture or painting. Our selections represent his best work in both arts. These are arranged, not in chronological order, but in a way which will lead the student from the subjects most familiar and easily understood to those which are more abstract and difficult.

ESTELLE M. HURLL.

New Bedford, Mass.
January, 1900.

CONTENTS AND LIST OF PICTURES

Portrait of Michelangelo. Attributed to Bugiardini. *Frontispiece.*

Note: All the pictures with the exception of the Cupid were made from photographs by Fratelli Alinari. The Cupid was photographed from the statue in the South Kensington Museum, London.

INTRODUCTION

I. ON MICHELANGELO'S CHARACTER AS AN ARTIST.

Michelangelo's place in the world of art is altogether unique. His supremacy is acknowledged by all, but is understood by a few only. In the presence of his works none can stand unimpressed, yet few dare to claim any intimate knowledge of his art. The quality so vividly described in the Italian word *terribilitá> is his predominant trait. He is one to awe rather than to attract, to overwhelm rather than to delight. The spectator must needs exclaim with humility, "Such knowledge is too wonderful for me; it is high, I cannot attain unto it." Yet while Michelangelo can never be a popular artist in the ordinary sense of the word, the powerful influence which he exercises seems constantly increasing. Year by year there are more who, drawn by the strange fascination of his genius, seek to read the meaning of his art.*

His subjects are all profoundly serious in intention. Life was no holiday to this strenuous spirit; it was a stern conflict with the powers of darkness in which such heroes as David and Moses were needed. Like the old Hebrew prophets, the artist poured out his soul in a vehement protest against evil, and a stirring call to righteousness.

Considered both as a sculptor and a painter, Michelangelo's one vehicle of expression was the human body. His works are "form-poems," through which he uttered [viii] his message to mankind. As he writes in one of his own sonnets,

> *"Nor hath God deigned to show himself elsewhere*
> *More clearly than in human forms sublime."*

In his art, says the critic Symonds, "a well-shaped hand, or throat, or head, a neck superbly poised on an athletic chest, the sway of the trunk above the hips, the starting of the muscles on the flank, the tendons of the ankle, the outline of the shoulder when the arm is raised, the backward bending of the loins, the curves of a woman's breast, the contours of a body careless in repose or strained for action, were all words pregnant with profoundest meaning, whereby fit utterance might be given to thoughts that raise man near to God."

Learning his first lessons in art of the Greeks, he soon possessed himself of the great principles of classic sculpture. Then he boldly struck out his own path; his was a spirit to lead, not to follow. With the subtle Greek sense of line and form, he united an entirely new motif. In contrast to the ideal of repose which was the leading canon of the Greeks, his chosen ideal was one of action. Moreover, he invariably fixed upon some decisive moment in the action he had to represent, a moment which suggests both the one preceding and the one following, and which gives us the whole story in epitome. Thus in the David we see preparation, aim, and action. It was a far cry from the elegant calm of the Greek god to the restless energy of this rugged youth.

Even with seated figures he followed the same principle. Moses and the Duke Giuliano are ready to rise to their feet if need be. In his frescoes we again find the same motif, – Adam rising to his feet in obedience to the Creator's summons, and Christ the Judge sweeping asunder the multitudes.

In his love of action and his passion for the human [ix] form lay the elements of his art most easily lending themselves to exaggeration. That the master did indeed permit himself to be carried beyond due limits in these matters is seen by comparing the grandeur of the Sistine ceiling with the mannerisms of the Last Judgment. The interval between was "the time of his best technical and spiritual creativeness," when he produced the statues of the Sacristy of S. Lorenzo.

It was characteristic of Michelangelo's impetuous nature to spend his enthusiasm upon the early stages of his work, and leave it unfinished. This unfinished effect of many of his marbles seems to bring us in closer touch with his methods as a sculptor. Nor is a rough surface here and there inharmonious with the rugged character of his conceptions. Moreover, as a critic [1] has pointed out, the polished and rough portions enhance each other, giving a variety in the light and shadow which is pictorial in effect.

[1] See notes on the Life of Michelangelo Buonarotti in the Blashfield-Hopkins edition of Vasari.

To a man of Michelangelo's austere temperament, intensely masculine in his predilections, the beauty of womanhood was not fully revealed. His sibyls can scarcely be counted as women; they belong to a world of their own, neither human nor divine. It was only in his few Madonnas that we can trace his feminine ideal, an ideal noble and dignified, rather than beautiful. The Madonna of the bas-relief is proud rather than tender, the Virgin of the Piet□s grand rather than lovely. These were works of his youth. Later in life, when he had known the blessing of a good woman's friendship, he developed a new ideal in the gentle and delicate womanhood of the Virgin of the Last Judgment.

Michelangelo has been compared to two great masters of dissimilar arts, Milton and Beethoven. There are [x] striking points of similarity in the men themselves, in stern uprightness of character, in scorn of the low and trivial, in lofty idealism. The art of all three is too far above the common level to be popular; it requires too much thinking to attract the superficial. In poetry, in music, and in sculpture, all three utter the profoundest truths of human experience, expressed in grand and solemn harmonies.

II. ON BOOKS OF REFERENCE.

The original materials for the study of Michelangelo's life and work are the two biographies by his contemporaries, Vasari and Condivi. Vasari's was the first of these (1550), and like the other portions of his "Lives of the Painters" contained many inaccuracies. It was to correct these that Condivi published his little book a few years later. This rival effort aroused Vasari's wrath, and after Michelangelo's death he issued an enlarged edition of his own book, unscrupulously incorporating all that was valuable in Condivi's work, and adding thereto many reminiscences of the master's life. The fame of Vasari's monumental work caused Condivi's little book to be entirely forgotten for long years, and it has been one of the tasks of modern scholarship to restore it to its true place. Even now, however, there is no available form of Condivi's biography for American readers, though Vasari's "Lives" in Mrs. Foster's translation is found in most libraries. The latest edition of Vasari, published in 1897, contains annotations by Mr. and Mrs. E.H. Blashfield, and A.A. Hopkins, which correct all the statements in the light of recent authorities.

Far more valuable even than the early biographies is the mass of existing documents of the Buonarotti family, including contracts, letters, poems, and memoranda, and containing data for a full and exact biography of the mas [xi] ter. Unfortunately, however, this great storehouse of material has been for all these centuries a sealed treasure, given up only little by little, to successive generations of scholars. When Hermann Grimm wrote his celebrated "Life of Michael Angelo" (in 1860), the only original material accessible to him was the collection of letters in the British Museum. His volumes are still read with interest and profit, though it is to be regretted that they should be reprinted without any editorial comments to connect formerly received opinions with later conclusions. John S. Harford's "Life of Michael Angelo Buonarotti" was published at about the same time as Grimm's work, that is, in 1857. It was in two volumes, and contained translations of many of Michelangelo's poems, as well as material about Savonarola, Vittoria Colonna, and Raphael. The work is found in the older libraries, and is well worth studying, as the latter portion is still valuable for all that refers to the architecture of St. Peter's.

Signor Gotti's "Vita," in 1875, was the first to profit to any considerable degree by documentary researches. The conclusions of this book are best known to the English-reading public through Charles Heath Wilson's "Life and Works of Michelangelo Buonarotti" (1876 and 1881), consisting of compilations from Gotti, to which are added original investigations of the Sistine frescoes, which are very valuable.

More privileged than any of his predecessors was John Addington Symonds, who, by special favor of the Italian government, was allowed to examine the Buonarotti collection in Florence, so long debarred to others. His "Life of Michelangelo Buonarotti" is therefore unique in being, as the sub-title announces, "based on studies in the archives of the Buonarotti family at Florence." It was published in 1893 in two large, finely illustrated volumes, and is taken as the latest authoritative word on the sub [xii] ject, a word singularly independent of others' conclusions, and influenced by an artistic and literary nature of rare sensitiveness.

To those who wish briefer notices of Michelangelo's life and work than any of these full biographies are recommended the chapters on Michelangelo in Kugler's "Handbook of the Italian Schools," in Mrs. Jameson's "Memoirs of the Italian Painters," in Frank Preston Stearns's "Midsummer of Italian Art," in Mrs. Oliphant's "Makers of Florence," and in Symonds's volume on "Fine Arts" in the series "Renaissance in Italy."

To understand more fully the character of the man Michelangelo, the student should read his sonnets. There is a complete collection translated by J.A. Symonds, while both Wordsworth and Longfellow have translated a few.

The life of Michelangelo has furnished material for two long poems by American writers, — Longfellow's drama, and the poem by Stuart Sterne. The former, which is annotated, is a well-balanced study of the great artist's career and ideals.

III. HISTORICAL DIRECTORY OF THE WORKS OF ART IN THIS COLLECTION.

Portrait frontispiece. An oil painting in The Hall of the Portraits of Old Masters, Uffizi Gallery, Florence. The authorship of the painting is not certainly known. Symonds says that "it may perhaps be ascribed with some show of probability to Bugiardini." Bugiardini was a friend of Michelangelo's youth and a fellow student in the gardens of the Medici. That later in life he painted a portrait of his distinguished friend we know from Vasari. Vasari tells us that the portrait showed a peculiarity in the right eye, and this fact lends probability to the identification of the Uffizi portrait with Bugiardini's work.

1. **Madonna and Child** , an unfinished bas-relief medallion, made, according to Vasari, during Michelangelo's residence in [xiii] Florence in 1501-1505. It was made for Bartolommeo Pitti. It is now in the National Museum (Bargello), Florence.

2. **David** , a statue made from a block of Carrara marble which had been spoiled by an unskilled sculptor. After it had lain useless in Florence for a century, a sculptor applied to the board of works of the cathedral for permission to use it. The board consulted Michelangelo and offered him the marble. He undertook to cut from it a single figure which would exactly use the block. The contract to make the statue of David was drawn up in 1501, and the statue was completed in 1504. Forty men were employed four days to remove it from the cathedral works to the Piazza della Signoria, where it was placed on the platform of the palace (Palazzo Vecchio), remaining in the open air more than three centuries. The weather was beginning to injure it, and it was removed in 1873 to the Academy of Fine Arts in Florence, where it now stands.

3. **Cupid.** Symonds gives the following account of the statue in the "Life of Michelangelo," published in 1893: "Discovered some forty years ago, hidden away in the cellars of the Gualfonda (Ruccellai) Gardens, Florence, by Professor Milanesi and the famous Florentine sculptor, Santarelli. On a cursory examination they both declared it to be a genuine Michelangelo. The left arm was broken, the right hand damaged, and the hair had never received the sculptor's final touches. Santarelli restored the arm, and the Cupid passed by purchase into the possession of the English nation." It is now in the Museum of South Kensington.

4. **Moses** , *a statue on the tomb commemorative of Julius II., [2] in the church of S. Pietro in Vincoli, Rome. At the beginning of Michelangelo's connection with Julius II., he made plans for a magnificent monumental tomb for this pope, to be ornamented with more than forty statues and to be of great size (34-1/2 ʋ23 feet). The fickleness of the Pope caused a continual series of disappointments in the progress of the work, which was finally abandoned for the frescoes of the Sistine Chapel. After the death of the Pope, his executors were even less zealous [xiv] for the completion of the tomb. A succession of contracts were made and broken, each one reducing the size and importance of the design. The artist was continually in demand for other work. Finally, in 1542, to leave him free for the services of the Pope, the completion of the tomb was put into other hands. The statue of Moses, with those of Rachel and Leah, is all that Michelangelo contributed to a work which had occupied his thoughts for nearly forty years. The setting of the Moses is in every way exceedingly unfavorable to a proper appreciation of the work.*

[2] *The Pope, Julius II., is buried at St. Peter's.*

5. **Holy Family** , *an oil painting belonging to the Florentine period 1501-1505, and painted for Angelo Doni. It is now in the Uffizi Gallery, Florence.*

6. **The Piet<si>** , *a marble group executed by the order of the Cardinal di San Dionigi according to a contract drawn up August 28, 1498. It was placed in the old basilica of St. Peter's (Rome), in a chapel dedicated to Our Lady of the Fever (Madonna della Febbre). In the present church of St. Peter's it occupies a side chapel, to which it gives its name, where it is placed so high that it is impossible to see it well, and where its beauty is disfigured by the bronze cherubs fastened above, holding a crown over the Virgin's head.*

7. **Christ Triumphant** , *a marble statue ordered by Bernardo Cencio (a canon of St. Peter's), Mario Scappuci, and Metello Varj dei Porcari for the church of S. Maria sopra Minerva, Rome, where it still stands. The deed was executed in 1514, specifying that the statue should be of marble, "life sized, naked, erect, with a cross in his arms." It appears from Michelangelo's correspondence that the work was finished by apprentices, first by Pietro Urbano, who did so badly that he was discharged and replaced by Federigo Frizzi. It was completed in 1521, when Michelangelo offered to make a new statue if it was not satisfactory. Varj, however, declared that*

the sculptor had "already made what could not be surpassed and was incomparable," so the statue was placed in position.

*8-12. **The Creation of Man, Jeremiah, Daniel, The Delphic Sibyl, the Cum栢 Sibyl** , frescoes on the ceiling of the Sistine Chapel, Rome, begun in 1508 at the order of the Pope [xv] Julius II. Michelangelo undertook the work reluctantly, as sculpture was his chosen art. The architect Bramante first made a scaffolding for the work, so clumsily constructed that Michelangelo replaced it by one of his own invention. Several Florentine painters were engaged as assistants, but, failing to satisfy the painter, returned. Julius II. often visited the chapel during the work, climbing to the scaffolding to see how it progressed. Impatient to see it, he gave orders to have the ceiling uncovered when but half finished. The first uncovering took place November 1, 1509. The work was completed October, 1512.*

*13-14. **Lorenzo de' Medici, Tomb of Giuliano de' Medici** , marble tombs first projected in 1520 or 1521, during the pontificate of Leo X. (formerly Giovanni de' Medici). The order was renewed by Clement VII., another Medici pope, in 1523. The work was carried on intermittently a number of years during which occurred the revolution, siege, and recapture of Florence. From 1530-1533 Michelangelo carried them to the point of completion in which they are now seen: they were never fully finished. The identity of the tombs was long a matter of doubt. Though Vasari had called the helmeted figure Lorenzo and the other Giuliano, there were critics, notably Grimm, who took the opposite view. In 1875 the sarcophagus of the helmeted figure was opened and evidence found proving it to be unquestionably the tomb of Lorenzo, as Vasari had said. Both tombs remain as originally placed in the new sacristy of the church of San Lorenzo, Florence.*

*15. **Central Figures of the Last Judgment** , a fresco painting on the wall of the Sistine Chapel, executed by the order of the Pope Paul III., who in 1535 appointed Michelangelo chief architect, sculptor, and painter at the Vatican. The work occupied several years and was completed in 1541.*

IV. COLLATERAL READINGS FROM LITERATURE.

IN CONNECTION WITH THE SEVERAL WORKS HERE REPRESENTED.

The Madonna and Child and the Holy Family: —

The Latin hymn, Mater Speciosa, by Jacobus de Benedictis, translated by Dr. Neale.

[xvi]

David: —

Arthur Penrhyn Stanley. History of the Jewish Church, Part II. Lectures XXII.-XXV.: David.

Robert Browning. Poem, Saul.

Psalm Twenty-three.

Cupid: —

Richard Crashaw. Poem, Cupid's Cryer; out of the Greek.

Edmund Gosse. Poem, Cupido Crucifixus.

Moses: —

Arthur Penrhyn Stanley. History of the Jewish Church, Part I, Lectures V.-VIII.: Moses.

Mrs. A.D.T. Whitney. The Open Mystery: A Reading of the Mosaic Story, Part IV.

The Song of Moses: Deuteronomy, chapter xxxii.

The Prayer of Moses: Psalm Ninety.

Cecil Frances Alexander. Poem, The Burial of Moses.

Sonnet on the statue of Moses by Giovanni Battista Felice Zappi, translated by J.A. Symonds (in Life of Michelangelo Buonarotti).

The Piet□#8212;

Latin hymn, Stabat Mater, by Jacobus de Benedictis, translated by Lord Lindsay, by General Dix or by Dr. Coles.

Christ Triumphant: —

Henryk Sienkiewicz. Quo Vadis, chapter lxix.

Frescoes of the Sistine Chapel, general impressions: —

Symonds. Renaissance in Italy, volume on the Fine Arts, chapter viii.: Life of Michael Angelo.

Taine. Italy, book iii., chapter ix.: Michael Angelo.

Andersen. The Improvisatore, chapter xii.: Allegri's Miserere, in the Sistine Chapel.

The Creation of Man: —

Milton. Paradise Lost, book VIII., lines 500-528.

Jeremiah: —

Lucy Larcom. Poem, The Weeping Prophet.

[xvii]

Daniel: —

Sir Edwin Arnold. Poem, The Feast of Belshazzar.

The Delphic Sibyl: —

Lord Houghton. Delphi, a poem included in Longfellow's collection of Poems of Places, volume on Greece.

The Cum栢 Sibyl: —

Virgil. Ƭeid, sixth book, translated by C.P. Cranch or by John Conington.

The Medicean Tombs, general impressions: —

Symonds. The Renaissance in Italy, volume on the Fine Arts, chapter viii.: Life of Michael Angelo.

Taine. Italy, book iii., chapter v.: The Florentine School of Art.

Mrs. Oliphant. The Makers of Florence, chapter xv.: Michael Angelo.

Rogers. Italy: poem on Florence.

Lorenzo de' Medici: —

Milton. Il Penseroso.

Tomb of Giuliano de' Medici: —

Charles Algernon Swinburne. Poem, In San Lorenzo.

The Last Judgment: —

The Latin hymn, Dies Irae, by Thomas de Celano, translated by General John E. Dix.

Alexander Dumas. Les Trois Maitres: Description of Last Judgment, translated by Esther Singleton in the compilation Great Pictures described by Great Writers.

The portrait of Michelangelo: —

C.P. Cranch. Michael Angelo Buonarotti, a poem read at a celebration of the 400th anniversary of his birth, included in Longfellow's collection of Poems of Places, volume on Italy.

[xviii]

V. OUTLINE TABLE OF THE PRINCIPAL EVENTS IN MICHELANGELO'S LIFE.

(Based on Symonds' Life of Michelangelo Buonarotti, to which the accompanying notes on pages refer.)

1475. Born at Caprese, March 6 (p. 4).

1488. Apprenticed to Domenico and David Ghirlandajo, April 1 (p. 12).

1489-1492. Under the patronage of Lorenzo the Magnificent, in the Casa Medici (p. 23).

1494, 1495. In Bologna, work on the tomb of St. Dominick (pp. 47, 48).

1495. Return to Florence, the Sleeping Cupid (pp. 50-52).

1496-1498. In Rome: —
The Bacchus (p. 58).
The South Kensington Cupid (p. 62).
The Piet□p. 69).

1500. A second visit to Rome (p. 80).

1501-1505. In Florence (p. 87).

1504. Statue of David (p. 96) taken from workshop, May 14;
arrived at Piazza Signoria, May 18;
set in place, June 8.

Commissioned in August to prepare cartoons for decoration of Hall in Palazzo Vecchio, on wall opposite to that assigned to Leonardo da Vinci (p. 119).

1505. Arrival in Rome to work under patronage of the Pope Julius II. (p. 126).

Preparations begun for work on tomb of Julius and trip to Carrara to select marbles (p. 129).

1506. His angry flight from Rome (p. 155).

Visit in Florence and completion of competitive cartoon (Battle of Pisa) for Palazzo Vecchio (p. 161).

Reconciliation with the Pope at Bologna, November (p. 186).

1506-1508. Residence in Bologna, and statue of Julius II. (pp. 187 and 195).

1508. Return to Florence, March (p. 197).

Thence to Rome by order of Julius II. (p. 198).

Frescoes of the Sistine Chapel begun (p. 206).

[xix] 1509. First uncovering of the Sistine Chapel ceiling, showing frescoes in the central space (pp. 209, 211).

1512. Sistine frescoes completed, October (p. 217).

1513. Death of Michelangelo's patron, Julius II., Feb. 21.

New contract for tomb, dated May 6 (p. 302).

1514. Contract for life size marble statue of Christ. Date of deed, June 14 (p. 305).

1516. Reduced plan for tomb of Julius II. (p. 320).

Visit to Carrara to quarry marble.

Suspension of work on tomb to make façade of church of S. Lorenzo (Florence) for Pope Leo X. (p. 323).

1518. Contract for façade of S. Lorenzo, Jan. 19 (p. 328).

1518, 1519. To and from Florence and Carrara for marble (pp. 331, 339, 341, 342).

1520. Façade of S. Lorenzo abandoned (p. 349).

1521. Work begun on tombs in sacristy of S. Lorenzo (p. 357).

Statue of Christ finished (pp. 306, 359).

Death of Michelangelo's patron, Leo X., Dec. 1.

1523. Fresh beginning of project of the Medicean tombs in sacristy of S. Lorenzo (p. 372).

1524. Vasari's apprenticeship with Michelangelo (p. 389).

1525. Work in Florence on Medicean tombs (p. 391).

1526. Work begun on Laurentian Library (p. 397).

1527, 1528. Uneventful years in Florence (p. 404).

1529. His services on the fortifications of S. Miniato, to defend Florence against the Medici (pp. 409, 412).

Flight from Florence to Venice, Sept. 21 (p. 416).

1530. Capitulation of Florence (p. 435).

Michelangelo in hiding (p. 437).

Resumption of work on Medicean tombs (p. 438).

1530-1533. Work on Medicean tombs (p. 447).

1532. New contract for tomb of Julius II. (p. 455).

1534. Death of Clement VII.

1535. Appointed chief architect, sculptor, and painter at the Vatican by Pope Paul III., Sept. 1 (vol. ii. p. 40).

1536-1537. Work on the Last Judgment (vol. ii. p. 43).

1538-1547. Friendship with Vittoria Colonna (vol. ii. pp. 93, 117, 125).

[xx] 1541. Last Judgment shown to the public, Christmas day (vol. ii. p. 58).

1542. Work assigned by Paul III. for frescoes in the Paulien Chapel (vol. ii. p. 69).

Michelangelo's last contract for tomb of Julius II. (vol. ii. pp. 40, 69, 73).

1544. Illness (vol. ii. pp. 183, 187).

1546. Michelangelo succeeds Antonio da Gallo as architect-in-chief at St. Peter's (vol. ii. p. 213).

1552. Invitation of Duke Cosimo de' Medici to return to Florence declined (vol. ii. pp. 289-291).

1556. Excursion to Spoleto (vol. ii. p. 303).

1557. Model for cupola of St. Peter's (vol. ii. p. 232).

1564. Death in Rome, Feb. 17 (vol. ii. p. 320).

VI. SOME OF MICHELANGELO'S FAMOUS ITALIAN CONTEMPORARIES.

Rulers.

Florentine Dukes : –

Lorenzo de' Medici, 1469-1492.

Piero de' Medici succeeded Lorenzo 1492, expelled from Florence 1493.

Alessandro de' Medici, made first hereditary duke of Florence 1531, assassinated 1537.

Cosimo de' Medici succeeded Alessandro, 1537-1574.

Popes : –

Sixtus IV., 1471-1484.

Innocent VIII., 1484-1492.

Alexander VI., 1492-1503.

Pius III., 1503-1503.

Julius II., 1503-1513.

Leo X., 1513-1522.

Hadrian VI., 1522-1523.

Clement VII., 1523-1534.

Paul III., 1534-1550.

Marcellus II., 1550-1555.

Paul IV., 1555-1555.

Pius IV., 1555-1559.

Pius V., 1559-1566.

Men of Letters.

Boiardo, 1434-1494, poet (Orlando Innamorato).

Ariosto, 1474-1533, poet (Orlando Furioso).

[xxi] Aretino (Venetian) 1492-1557, poet.

Francesco Berni, 1496-1535, burlesque poet.

Bandello, 1480-1562, novelliero.

Sannazaro, 1458-1530, poet (Arcadia).

Niccolo Machiavelli, 1469-1527, author of The Prince.

Gucciardini, 1483-1540, historian.

Tasso, 1544-1595, poet (Gerusalemme Liberata).

Group centring about Lorenzo the Magnificent in Florence.

Cristoforo Landino, 1424-1504, tutor of Lorenzo, and professor of Latin Literature.

Bartolommeo Scala, 1430-1497, chancellor of Florence.

Luigi Pulci, 1431-1487, writer of burlesque epic Il Morgante Maggiore, and intimate friend of Lorenzo and Poliziano.

Marsilio Ficino, 1433-1499, president of Academy in 1463, translator of Plato and Plotinus.

Angelo Poliziano, 1454-1494, tutor of Lorenzo's children, and professor of Greek and Latin Literature in University of Florence.

Giovanni Pico della Mirandola, 1463-1494, published 900 theses at Rome in defence of Platonic mysticism.

Group in Rome:—

Pietro Bembo, 1470-1547, made cardinal in 1539, master of Latin style and also writer in Italian.

Jacopo Sadoleto, 1477-1547, made cardinal in 1536, writer of Latin verses, moral treatises, and commentary on Romans.

Egidio Canisio, 1470-1532, made cardinal in 1457, Latin orator and writer on philosophy, history, and theology.

Paolo Giovio, 1483-1552, bishop of Nocera 1528, historian and biographer.

Baldassare Castiglione, 1478-1529, diplomatist and scholar.

Gian Francesco Pico della Mirandola, 1470-1533, author of life of Savonarola.

Jerome Aleander, 1480-1542, made cardinal in 1536, librarian at Vatican.

Marcus Musurus, 1470-1517, lecturer in Gymnasium Caballini Montis.

[xxii] Joannes Lascaris, 1445-1535, superintendent of Greek press established in Rome by Leo X.
Riario, Giulio de' Medici, Bibbiena, Petrucci, Farnese, Alidosi, Gonzaga, cardinals and patrons of literature.

PAINTERS.

Ghirlandajo,	1449-1495?	Florentine
Verrocchio,	1435-1488	"
Leonardo da Vinci,	1452-1519	"
Bartolommeo,	1475-1517	"
Francesco Granacci,	1477-1543 (friend of Michelangelo)	"
Giuliano Bugiardini,	1475-1554 (friend of Michelangelo)	"
Raphael,	1483-1520	"
Andrea del Sarto,	1486-1531	"
Sebastiano del Piombo,	1485-1547	"
Giorgio Vasari,	1512-1574	"
Giovanni Bellini,	1428-1516	Venetian
Giorgione,	1477-1510	"
Titian,	1477-1576	"
Tintoretto,	1518-1594	"
Paolo Veronese,	1528-1588	"
Perugino,	1446-1523	Umbrian
Bazzi,	1477-1549	Sienese
Baldassare Peruzzi,	1481-1536 (also architect)	"

Domenico Beccafumi,	1486-1551	"
Mantegna,	1431-1506	Mantuan
Francia,	1450-1518	Bolognese
Correggio,	1494-1534	Emilian

MISCELLANEOUS.

Savonarola, 1452-1498, prior of monastery of S. Marco, Florence, preacher, reformer, martyr.

Marc' Antonio, 1487-1539, engraver.

Bramante, 1444-1514, architect of St. Peter's.

Antonio da San Gallo, 1485-1546, architect of St. Peter's.

Christopher Columbus, 1436 or 1446-1506, discoverer.

Aldo Manuzio (Teobaldo Mannucci), 1450-1515, printer, established press at Venice 1490.

Vittoria Colonna, 1490-1547, poet.

THE MADONNA AND CHILD

About two thousand years ago a babe was born in the little Jud柘village of Bethlehem whose life was to change all history. His name was Jesus, and every Christian country now takes his birth as a standard from which to reckon time. When we speak of the year 1900, we are counting the number of years that have passed since that event. [3] To make this clear we sometimes add the initials a.d., standing for the Latin words, Anno Domini, meaning in the year of our Lord. To go still farther back we speak of an event as so many years b.c. or Before Christ.

[3] To be perfectly exact we must always add four years to a date to get the full length of time passed since the birth of Christ, as a mistake has been made in the calculation.

The infant Jesus came to his mother Mary as a peculiar treasure. Before his birth she had had a vision of an angel telling her that her son was to reign over a great kingdom. She felt that there was a great and solemn mystery in his life.

At the time he was born, Bethlehem happened to be crowded with people who had come there to pay their taxes. When Mary and her husband Joseph went to the inn, there was no room for them, and the baby was laid in a manger used to feed cattle. [2] This was a humble cradle for one destined to be a king; but the mother did not think too much of outward things. Her confidence in her son's greatness was not to be shaken by trifles like this.

The new-born babe was soon sought out. First came some shepherds asking to see him, because, while watching their sheep at night, they had had a vision of angels telling them that a Saviour was born in Bethlehem. Still stranger visitors were some wise men from the East, who said they had seen a star which signified to them the birth of a king. They brought the babe royal gifts of gold and frankincense and myrrh, and returned on their way well pleased with the success of their journey.

When the babe was about a month old he was carried up to the great city of Jerusalem, where, according to the religious custom of the Jews, he was to be offered or presented to the Lord, in the temple. Here a saintly old man named Simeon took him in his arms, with some strange words of prophecy of the salvation which this child was to bring to the world.

All these things made a deep impression upon Mary, and she was a proud and devoted mother. Day by day she watched her child grow "strong in spirit, filled with wisdom; and the grace of God was upon him." It is said that

> "All mothers worship little feet,
> And kiss the very ground they've trod,"

and this mother had special cause for child worship.

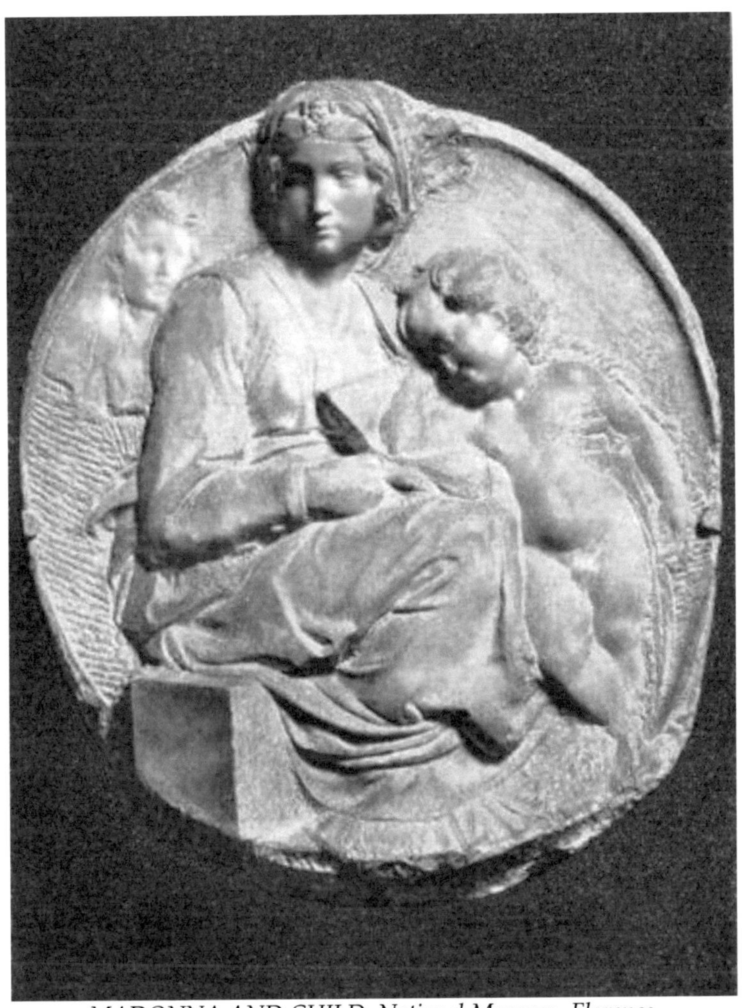

MADONNA AND CHILD. National Museum, Florence.

The Italians always refer to the mother of Jesus [5] as the Madonna, which is the old Italian way of addressing a lady. This representation of the Madonna and Child makes us understand better what the two were to each other. The confiding way in which the boy leans against his mother's knee shows the love between them. The mother looks like a queen; on her well-

poised head she wears a headdress something like a crown. As the mother of a prince she bears her honors proudly.

On her lap is the book from which she has been reading. The child seems dreaming of the wonderful words he has heard, as he rests his cheek on his little hand, his elbow bent across the open page. A thoughtful mood is upon them both, and there is something wistful in the boy's attitude. The message they have read must indeed be a solemn one. Perhaps it is something which recalls to the mother the promise of the angel in foretelling the birth of Jesus. She thinks of the great honors that are to be his, and also of the sacrifices by which they must be won. The book may be open at the words of one of those old Hebrew prophets who longed for the coming of the Redeemer. There is a verse in the prophecy of Isaiah, which speaks of a child upon whose shoulders the government shall rest. [4] The writer tells some of the many names by which he shall be called, and we may imagine this mother and child going over together these strange titles: "Wonderful, Counsellor, The Mighty God, The Everlasting Father, The Prince of Peace."

[6]

[4] Isaiah, chapter ix. verse 6.

Our illustration is from a bas-relief by Michelangelo, and as we examine it closely we discover that the sculptor's work was left unfinished. The rough marks of the chisel are still seen on the surface of the marble. A child's figure in the background is quite indistinct. Probably it was intended for the boy St. John the Baptist, the cousin of Jesus. The child Jesus himself is by no means completed; his right arm is only faintly indicated.

As we shall learn from other examples of sculpture in this book, [5] Michelangelo often neglected to carry his work to completion. He was so possessed with his ideas that he could not work fast enough in sketching them on the marble, but after this, it did not matter so much to him about the finishing. He had done enough to show his meaning.

[5] Note particularly the Cupid on page 15, and the tomb of Giuliano de' Medici on page 81.

There are reasons for liking such work all the better for being unfinished. Some of the most delightful stories ever written, like those of Hawthorne, leave something at the end still unexplained. The reader's imagination is then free to go on forever exploring the mystery, and inventing new situations. So in this bas-relief, the great sculptor does not work out the details, but allows us to exercise our own fancy upon them. He sketches his thought in a few noble lines, and each may round out for himself the completed ideal.

[7]

II

DAVID

Long ago in the country of Palestine lived a lad named David, who kept his father's sheep. His free life out of doors made him strong and manly beyond his years. The Israelites were at this time at war with the Philistines, and David's quick wit and indomitable courage fitted him to play an important part in the issue of the war.

The Philistine army contained a giant named Goliath, described as "six cubits and a span" in height. That is over ten feet; but perhaps his terrible appearance, in all his armor, made him taller than he really was.

One day this giant came out from his army and made a proposal to the Israelites: [6] "Choose you a man for you, and let him come down to me. If he be able to fight with me, and to kill me, then will we be your servants: but if I prevail against him and kill him, then shall ye be our servants, and serve us." Every day, morning and evening for forty days, the Philistine stood forth and repeated his challenge, yet in vain. Saul, the king, and all Israel, were "dismayed and greatly afraid."

[6] 1 Samuel, chapter xvii. verses 8, 9.

Now it happened that David's three elder brothers [8] were in the Israelite army, and one day their father sent him to them with a present of some provisions. While the lad was talking with his brothers, Goliath came out with his usual call of defiance. David listened with wonder and indignation. "Who is this Philistine?" he asked scornfully, "that he should defy the armies of the living God?" The brothers were angry at what they thought foolish bravado on the part of David; but there were others who reported his words to Saul, who forthwith sent for the lad. Then David amazed the king by boldly offering to go and fight with the Philistine.

"And Saul said to David, 'Thou art not able to go against this Philistine to fight with him: for thou art but a youth, and he a man of war from his

youth.' And David said unto Saul, 'Thy servant kept his father's sheep, and there came a lion, and a bear, and took a lamb out of the flock: And I went out after him, and smote him, and delivered it out of his mouth: and when he arose against me, I caught him by his beard, and smote him, and slew him. Thy servant slew both the lion and the bear.... The Lord that delivered me out of the paw of the lion, and out of the paw of the bear, he will deliver me out of the hand of this Philistine.' And Saul said unto David, 'Go, and the Lord be with thee.'

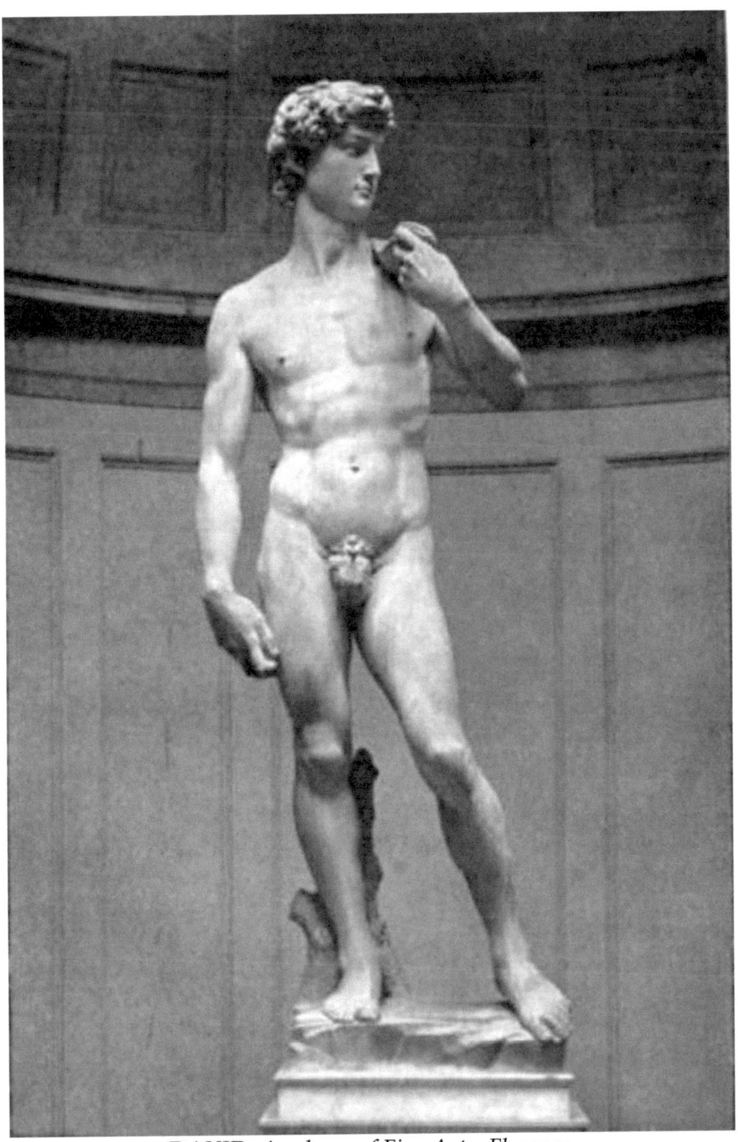

DAVID. *Academy of Fine Arts, Florence.*

"And Saul armed David with his armour, and he put an helmet of brass upon his head; also he armed him with a coat of mail. And David girded his

sword upon his armour, and he assayed to go; for [11] he had not proved it. And David said unto Saul, 'I cannot go with these; for I have not proved them.' And David put them off him. And he took his staff in his hand and chose him five smooth stones out of the brook,... and his sling was in his hand: and he drew near to the Philistine....

"And when the Philistine looked about, and saw David, he disdained him: for he was but a youth, and ruddy, and of a fair countenance.... And the Philistine said to David, 'Come to me, and I will give thy flesh unto the fowls of the air, and to the beasts of the field.' Then said David to the Philistine, 'Thou comest to me with a sword, and with a spear, and with a shield: but I come to thee in the name of the Lord of hosts, the God of the armies of Israel, whom thou hast defied. This day will the Lord deliver thee into mine hand; and I will smite thee, and take thine head from thee.' ...

"And it came to pass, when the Philistine arose, and came and drew nigh to meet David, that David hasted, and ran toward the army to meet the Philistine. And David put his hand in his bag, and took thence a stone, and slang it, and smote the Philistine in his forehead, that the stone sunk into his forehead; and he fell upon his face to the earth. So David prevailed over the Philistine with a sling and with a stone, and smote the Philistine, and slew him; but there was no sword in the hand of David. Therefore David ran, and stood upon the Philistine, and took his sword, and drew it out of the sheath [12] thereof, and slew him, and cut off his head therewith. And when the Philistines saw their champion was dead, they fled." [7]

[7] 1 Samuel, chapter xvii. verses 33-51.

This heroic adventure of David is the subject of Michelangelo's statue. The shepherd, having thrown off the king's armor, advances naked and unhampered, carrying only the sling flung across his back. The large muscular hand hanging by his side holds the piece of wood on which the sling is hung. It is the hand that wrenched the lamb from the lion's mouth and then seized the king of beasts himself by the beard. The left hand, poised on the shoulder, holds the centre of the sling where it bulges with the pebble. The youth scans the enemy keenly, marking the spot at which to aim. In another moment the pebble will be speeding on its way. His air of confidence makes us sure of the victory. Determination like this must win the day.

Critics of sculpture tells us that the statue of David must have been studied from a model of the age which Michelangelo imagined as that of the shepherd lad at this time. The figure is that of a growing youth, and alt-

hough it is therefore not so beautiful as a type of perfectly developed man-hood, it has a rugged strength which makes it one of the sculptor's most interesting works.

[13]

III

CUPID

In the mythology of ancient Greece there is no more popular figure than the little god of love, Eros, more commonly known by the Latin name Cupid. He was supposed to be the son of Venus, the goddess of love and beauty, whom he attended. He was never without his bow and quiver of arrows. Whoever was hit by one of his magic darts straightway fell in love. The wound was at once a pain and a delight. Some traditions say that he shot blindfolded, – his aim seemed often so at random. Sometimes the one whom he wounded was apparently least susceptible to love. Indeed, Cupid had the reputation of being rather a mischievous fellow, fond of pranks.

One of these was at the expense of Apollo, the great sun god. Apollo was himself a mighty archer, and had slain with his arrows the python of Delphi. Proud of his victory, he mocked at the little god of love, advising him to leave his arrows for the warlike, and content himself with the torch of love. Cupid, vexed at the taunt, replied threateningly, "Thine arrows may strike all things else, Apollo, but mine shall strike thee." So saying he drew from his quiver two arrows, one of gold, to excite love, [14] and one of lead, to repel it. With the golden one he shot Apollo through the heart, with the leaden he shot the nymph Daphne. So Apollo became nearly mad with love for Daphne, but the maid fled from him with horror. He pursued her, and when he was close upon her, she turned into a laurel-tree.

Cupid continued to work havoc with his arrows. Even his mother Venus could not escape their power. One day, when frolicking with her boy, she was wounded by one of the darts, and before the wound healed she saw and loved Adonis. When that youth was killed in a struggle with a wild boar, she was inconsolable.

Another romantic tragedy for which Cupid was responsible was the love between Hero and Leander. These two young people lived in towns on opposite sides of the Hellespont. Leander was one day worshipping in the temple of Venus, in Hero's town, Sestos, when he saw Hero, and was at that moment shot by Cupid's arrow. His love was returned, and every night he swam across the channel to see his lady love, until one night a tempest arose, and he was drowned. The waves bore his body to the shore, where Hero found him, and in her despair threw herself into the sea and was also drowned.

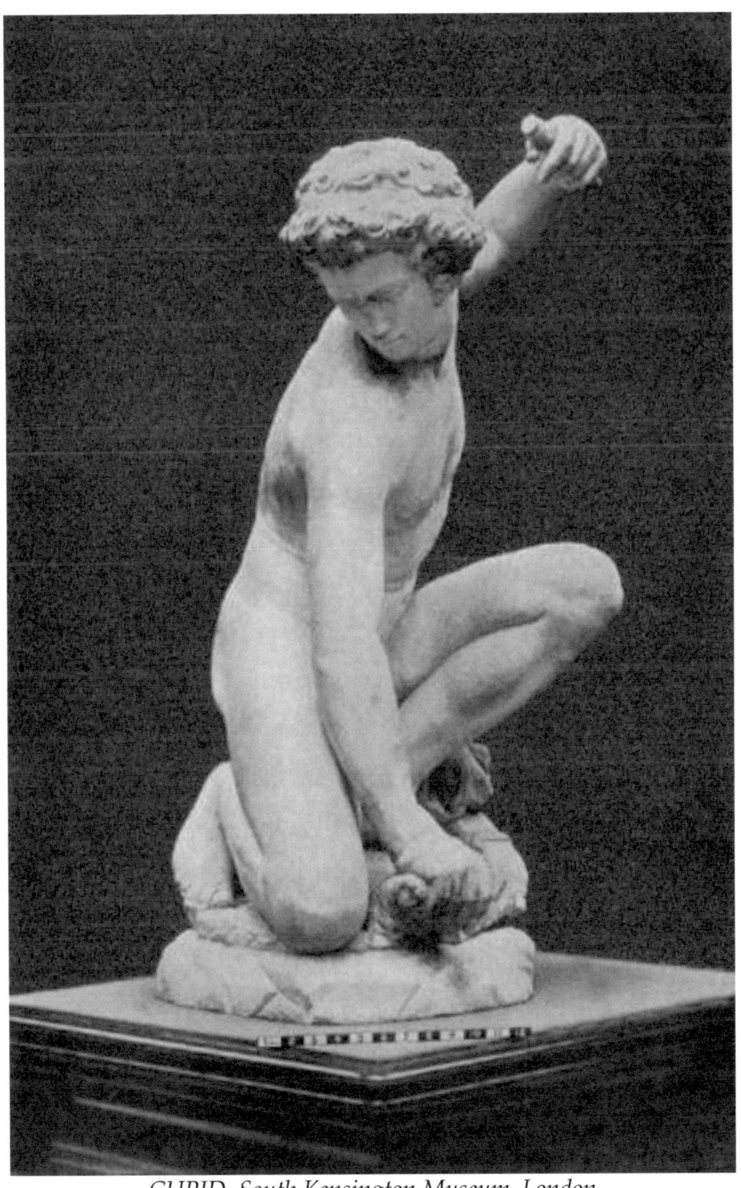

CUPID. *South Kensington Museum, London*

Such legends as these were dear to the hearts of the Greeks. Their poets and artists were very fond of the subject of Cupid. Now Michelangelo's early artistic training was under the influence of the Greek culture. He was an inmate of the household of Lorenzo de' Medici, who was an ardent lover of all [17] that was beautiful in Greek art and literature. At the table of the prince the youth must often have heard the old Greek myths related, and in the gardens he saw splendid Greek marbles. It was natural, then, that among his early works in sculpture he should choose the subject of Cupid. His idea was, however, his own, and was not at all such as a Greek would have imagined. Classic art always represented the god of love as a merry little winged boy, while in this statue he is seen as a well-grown youth. His face is strong and masterful, instead of innocently gay.

He has dropped on one knee to take an arrow from the ground. In his raised left hand he holds the bow, of which we see only a portion. His left leg is bent in position to rise again. Like David, he has an abundance of bushy hair crowning his handsome head; his straight brows and set mouth show the same determination of character. He stands for love which is determined to win, for love which conquers every obstacle, for love which is unerring in aim. It is a much nobler conception than the mere passing fancy of which the old myth speaks. Michelangelo was one who believed that

> *"Love betters what is best,*
> *Even here below, but more in heaven above." [8]*

So he put into a pagan fancy a new and higher meaning.

[8] one of Michelangelo's sonnets translated by Wordsworth.

To understand fully the qualities of this work of art, one ought to see it from many points of view, [18] and study the lines. The long curve of the right arm follows the curve of the right leg from hip to knee. The bend of the left arm repeats the line made by the bend of the left leg. The two extended arms together form a long line arching like the curve of a bow.

From every standpoint all the lines are beautiful and harmonious. This was the secret the Greeks had taught the young Italian sculptor. In other respects he was entirely original. Cupid, like David, is in an attitude of action. In another moment he will move. This was quite different from the Greek sculpture, which always gives an impression of repose.

Note. – There is a difference of opinion among critics as to the subject of the statue at South Kensington. Heath Wilson considered it an Apollo. The writer has followed Symonds in calling it Cupid.

The size of the statue may be calculated from the foot rule which lies across the pedestal in the picture.

[19]

IV

MOSES

In Michelangelo's statue of Moses the great Hebrew leader is represented at the height of his career. He was a prophet, a poet, a military commander, and a statesman. The story of his life will show how all these qualities could be combined in one person.

At the time of his birth his people were in slavery to the Egyptians, who cruelly oppressed them. Their numbers were increasing so rapidly that it was feared they would soon outnumber their masters. So the command went forth to drown every boy baby. Now the mother of Moses had no mind to lose her boy, and "when she could not longer hide him, she took for him an ark of bulrushes, and daubed it with slime and with pitch, and she put the child therein and laid it in the flags by the river's brink. And his sister stood afar off, to know what would be done to him." [9]

[9] Exodus, chapter ii. verses 3, 4, Revised Version.

Then a strange thing happened. The princess came to the river with her maids for a bath, and finding the babe, was touched by his cries. The sister came up as if by chance, and asked if she should seek a Hebrew nurse for the child, and when [20] the princess said Yes, she went straight for her mother.

So Moses was adopted by an Egyptian princess, yet he was nurtured in infancy by his own mother. This explains why, with all the Egyptian learning acquired at court, he had still the religious training of a Jew, and when he grew to manhood he was full of sympathy for the wrongs of his people. One day he saw an Egyptian smiting a Hebrew, and in his wrath he slew the Egyptian on the spot. News of the deed came to Pharaoh the king, and

Moses fled into a place called Midian. Here for forty years he lived a quiet pastoral life as a shepherd for Jethro, whose daughter he had married.

Then came the divine call. He was alone with his sheep on the mountainside, when he heard a voice saying, "Come now and I will send thee unto Pharaoh, that thou mayest bring forth my people the children of Israel out of Egypt,... and I will bring you up out of the affliction of Egypt unto the land of the Canaanites ... unto a land flowing with milk and honey." [10] Thus Moses became the leader of his people in their exodus, or departure from Egypt.

[10] Exodus, chapter iii verses 10 and 17.

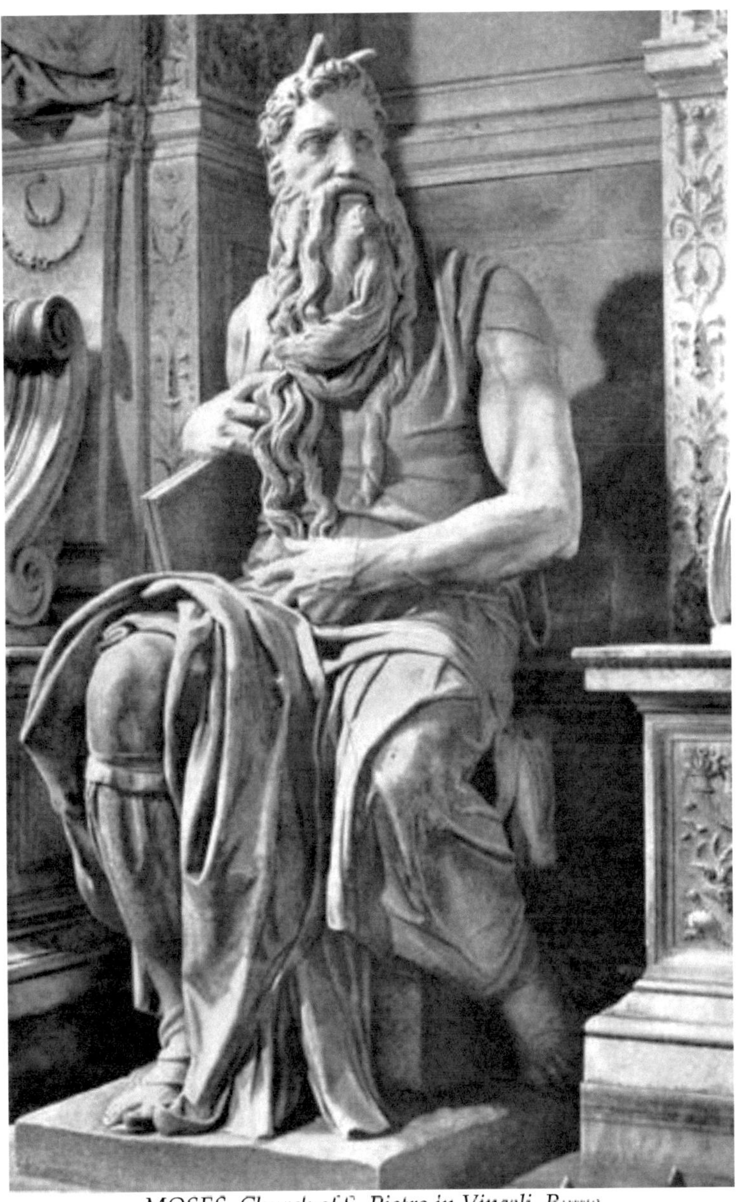

MOSES. *Church of S. Pietro in Vincoli, Rome*

After many strange experiences, the great company of emigrants made the passage of the Red Sea in safety, and Moses showed his poetic gifts in a song of triumph. Many years of slavery had taken the spirit out of the Hebrews, and they needed a wise head and a firm hand to govern them. Moses [23] had both, and he was, besides, a man of God. Going apart from them for a season of divine communion on the mountain, he spent forty days in preparation for a system of government. On his return he brought with him two tables of stone, inscribed with the ten great commandments, which are at the foundation of right character. He had also detailed directions for their daily conduct, and for their religious ceremonial.

The people for whose good all these plans were made were in the mean time discouraged by the long absence of their leader. They had no idea how much he was doing for them, and in their folly they forgot his teachings, and began to practise the idolatrous customs they had seen in Egypt. On descending the mountain, Moses found them worshipping the golden image of a calf. It is not to be wondered at that, as the historian says, [11] "Moses' anger waxed hot, and he cast the tables out of his hands, and brake them beneath the mount."

[11] Exodus, chapter xxxii. verse 19.

Again Moses went up into the mount for communion with God, and again two tables of stone were inscribed with the ten commandments, to replace those which had been destroyed. Again, also, he was gone forty days, and this time he was given a mysterious revelation of the goodness of God.

Thus it was that when he came down the people were afraid to come near, for [12] "the skin of his face shone," or "put forth beams," as the expression [24] reads in some Bible translations. In the old Latin version made by Jerome in the fifth century, and known as the Vulgate, translated into what is now called the Douay Bible, we read that "Moses' face was horned." This is why all the old artists, who were guided by the Vulgate, represented Moses with horns. These horns became, as it were, symbols of Moses' inspiration as a prophet.

[12] Ibid., chapter xxxiv. verse 30. See Revised Version.

Michelangelo followed the prevailing custom in using these curious symbols. The long curling beard gives his hero the aspect of a poet. The tables of stone show him to be a law-giver. But of all the qualities of this many-sided man seen in the great statue, the most conspicuous are his qualities of leadership, — the keen glance, the commanding air, the alert attitude, the determined look. He seems ready to spring to his feet if occasion demands. We see also something of his faults, of the impulsive anger which slew the Egyptian, and dashed in pieces the tables of stone, and of the arrogance which cost him the privilege of entering Canaan.

He was not permitted to see his labors carried to completion, but on the borders of Canaan "went up into the mountain of Nebo,... and died there in the land of Moab, according to the word of the Lord. And he buried him in a valley ... over against Beth-peor; but no man knoweth of his sepulchre unto this day."

[25]

V

THE HOLY FAMILY

The pictures we have thus far studied in this collection are reproductions of works of sculpture. This is the art which Michelangelo loved best. He was, however, a painter also, and in the later years of his life he was even drawn into architecture. Painting was the first art he studied, but he soon laid it aside for sculpture, and after that returned to it from time to time throughout his life.

This picture of the Holy Family is from an oil painting. It shows us a glimpse of the home life of the child Jesus. We have already seen in the bas-relief of the Madonna and Child how thoughtful a mood was sometimes upon the mother and her boy. In this picture they are making merry together. The mother, seated on the ground, tosses the boy with her strong arms, for her husband Joseph to catch. She is a beautiful woman, large, and full of life and vigor. The boy is a healthy, happy child, with perfect confidence in his mother. He rests his fat little hands on her head to steady himself.

Joseph, bald and gray, takes the play a little more seriously, as he gently lifts the boy from the mother's arms. He has a special care for the child. It was he who was warned by an angel in a dream [26] that it was dangerous to remain in Jud栢 It was he who "took the young child and his mother by night and departed into Egypt." [13] It was he again who duly brought them back to their native country when the cruel king was dead who had *threatened the child's life. After the return from Egypt Joseph and his family settled in the little town of Nazareth, where he followed the trade of a carpenter.*

[13] Matthew, chapter ii. verses 13, 14.

Now Jesus had a cousin, a boy who was not far from the same age. His name was John, and his mission in life was closely connected with that of Jesus. He was to grow up a great preacher, and finally to lead people to Jesus himself. His parents knew before his birth, from an angelic visitation, that he was to be a prophet. His mother Elizabeth, and Mary the mother of Jesus, used to talk together, before their children were born, of the strange future in store for them. We like to think that the two boys grew up as companions and playmates.

It is this little boy John who is seen in the back of the picture, at the right, coming up as if to join the child Jesus in his romp. We see his eager little face, with the long hair blown back from it, just above the coping stone surrounding the garden inclosure which the Holy Family occupy. He carries over his left shoulder a slender reed cross, such as is given him in all the old works of art as a symbol of his prophetic character.

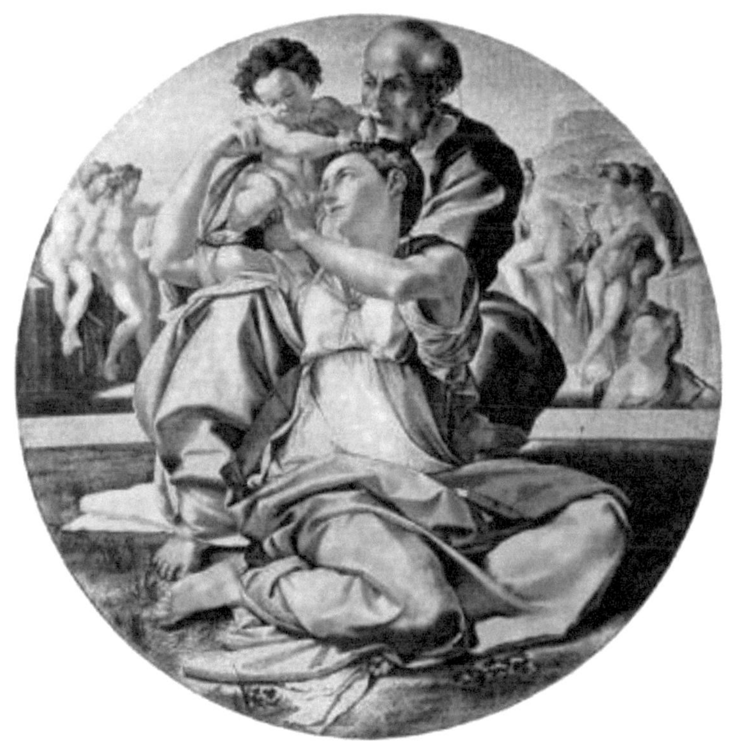

THE HOLY FAMILY. *Uffizi Gallery, Florence.*

Please click here for a modern color image

You may say when you look at the picture that [29] this is such a group as you might see any day in some Tuscan village. The people are indeed very plainly of the peasant class, and the artist did not go far out of his way to find his figures. Perhaps he thought this was after all the best way to show that the Holy Family was not unlike other families in enjoying the simple pleasures of home life. We may feel a closer sense of kinship with them on that account.

In studying the artistic qualities of this picture we have to remember that Michelangelo was more of a sculptor than a painter, and that he went to work upon a painting with the same methods he used in marble. The central figures are grouped in a solid mass as if for a bas-relief, as we may see by comparing this illustration with that of the Madonna and Child. The mother's arms are so "modelled," to use a critical term, that they seem to start out from the canvas "in the round," just as if cut from marble. The folds of her dress, as well as those of Joseph's garment, are arranged in the long beautiful lines artists call "sculpturesque."

The sculptor's methods are also plainly seen in the peculiarity of his background. In a picture of this kind most painters would have painted there a landscape, but Michelangelo did nothing of the kind. Instead there is a semicircular parapet upon which five slender unclothed youths are playing together. Three sit upon the wall and two lean against it.

The figures bear no relation to the story of the [30] picture. They are introduced merely for the sake of decoration. To Michelangelo there was nothing so beautiful in decoration as the human form. The lines made by different positions of the body trace patterns more beautiful, he thought, than any arabesques. The Greeks had the same idea when they decorated the pediments of their temples with bas-reliefs of nude figures. Applying this principle of sculpture to his painting, Michelangelo arranged these boys so that their slender limbs intertwine in graceful patterns, making a decorative background to fill in the picture. The lightness and delicacy of the design heighten the effect of solidity in the figures of the foreground, giving them the prominence of figures in relief.

[31]

VI

THE PIET

In the busy years of Christ's ministry we do not read of his often being with his mother Mary. He was going about the country preaching and healing, and gave himself wholly to his mission. Yet we know that the love between mother and son was constant and unchanging. From beginning to end she always had confidence in his power, and his tender care for her was among his last thoughts.

On the dreadful day of the Crucifixion, the mother was found standing by the cross, with her sister and Mary Magdalene. "When Jesus therefore saw his mother, and the disciple standing by, whom he loved [that is, St. John], he saith unto his mother, Woman, behold thy son! Then saith he to *the disciple, Behold thy mother! And from that hour that disciple took her unto his own home." [14]*

[14] John, chapter xix. verses 26, 27.

We can imagine the mother's anguish in seeing her son suffer this cruel and ignominious death. He had lived only to do good, and now he was dying an innocent sacrifice to his enemies. At such a moment the mother might truly feel that a sword was piercing her soul, as the old man Simeon [15] had once prophesied of her, many years before.

[15] Luke, chapter ii. verse 35.

[32]

> *"Wearied was her heart with grieving,*
> *Worn her breast with sorrow heaving,*
> *Through her soul the sword had passed.*

> *"Ah! how sad and broken-hearted*
> *Was that blessed mother, parted*
> *From the God-begotten One!*

> *"How her loving heart did languish*
> *When she saw the mortal anguish*
> *Which o'erwhelmed her peerless Son." [16]*

[16] From Stabat Mater.

Time passed, and Jesus now being dead, his friends were permitted by the governor to remove him from the cross. Joseph of Arimathea took the lead, as he was to lay the body in a new sepulchre recently made in his garden. Nicodemus was also there, bringing linen and spices for the burial, and the loving women lingered to see these preparations.

We can imagine how they might all stand aside to make room for the mother Mary. Perhaps, indeed, they would withdraw a little way to leave her for a moment alone with her son. The years seem to melt away, and again she gathers him in her lap as when he was a babe. All the motherly tenderness which she has had long pent up in her heart now overflows. If she has sometimes felt a little lonely that in his manhood he no longer needed her care, she forgets it now. He is still her child.

The marble group by Michelangelo interprets such a moment for us. The Italians call the subject the Piet Owhich means compassion, but the name scarcely expresses all the emotions of the mother. [35] She seems as strong and young as when she brooded over her babe in the Bethlehem manger. "Purity enjoys eternal youth" was the sculptor's explanation to those who objected.

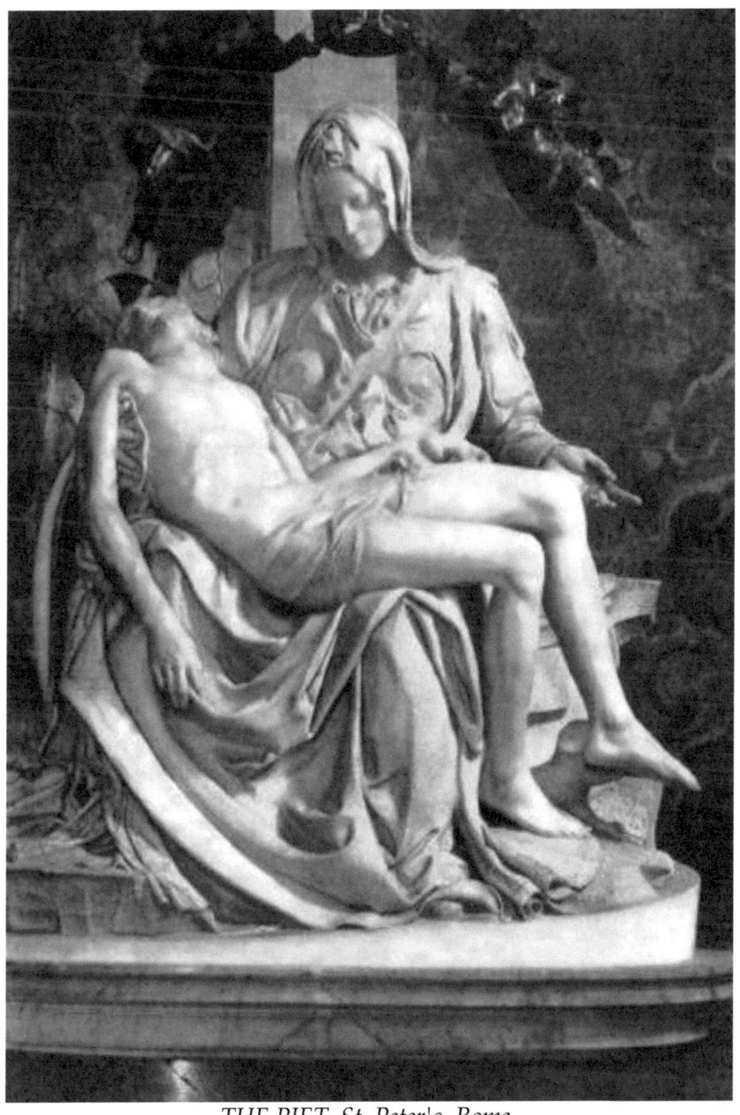

THE PIET. St. Peter's, Rome.

*Across her capacious, motherly lap lies the slender, youthful figure of the
dead Christ. The head falls back, and the limbs are relaxed in death. Suffer-
ing has left no trace on his face. The nail prints in hands and feet, and the*

scar in the side, are the only signs of his crucifixion. The delicately moulded body is beautiful in repose.

The mother seems to find mysterious comfort in gazing upon her son.
Perhaps his death has opened her eyes to the meaning of his life. If this is
so, she cannot grieve. He has finished the work given him to do, and death
is the beginning of immortality. So sorrow gives place to resignation. She
is again the proud mother. The fond hopes with which she watched his
childhood have been more than fulfilled. She extends her hand in a gesture
which seems to say, "Behold and see."

It is said that certain Lombards, passing through the church where the
Piet□tood, ascribed the work to a Milanese sculptor named Cristoforo
Solari. Michelangelo, having overheard them, shut himself up in the chapel, and chiselled his name upon the girdle which crosses the Madonna's
breast and supports her flowing garments. His name is not found on any of
his other works, and we can understand why he felt proud of such a mas-
terpiece. Though made when on the very threshold of his career, it [36] was
never surpassed even in his later years. Some other artist afterwards designed the two little bronze cherubs who hold a crown over the Madonna's
head. They are quite out of harmony with the impressive dignity of the
figures below.

Michelangelo's early love of Greek sculpture taught him many lessons,
which were worked out in this group. It has, first of all, that perfect repose
which was the leading trait in classic art. There is nothing strained or
violent in the positions. Besides this, the figures are so arranged that on all
sides, as in a Greek statue, the lines are beautiful and harmonious.

But the subject itself is one which would have been too sad for the pleas-
ure-loving Greek. To the pagan the thought of death was something to be
avoided. Michelangelo's statue teaches the highest lesson of religious
faith, – the beauty of resigned sorrow and the sublimity of sacrificing love.

[37]

VII

CHRIST TRIUMPHANT

(Cristo Risorto)

The character of Christ is so many-sided that when trying to fancy how he looked while he lived in the world, everyone has probably a different thought uppermost. The business man and the lawyer may imagine the keen, searching glance which he turned upon those who tried to entangle him with hard questions. A loving woman thinks rather of the compassionate look with which he greeted the sisters of Lazarus when they came to tell him that their brother was dead. The physician may wonder how he looked when he spoke the commanding words to those whom he healed.

Others dwell upon his sufferings as the Man of Sorrows, and often think how sad he looked when he referred to the disciple who should betray him. Lovers of nature like to imagine the look of pleasure on his face in seeing the lilies growing in the field, or the expression of eager inquiry with which he asked the fishermen what luck they had had. Every boy and girl likes best to think of him smiling upon the children, whom he called to him and took in his arms.

Now when an artist makes an ideal representation [38] of Christ, he tries to show us as many as possible of these elements of character combined in one figure. So we may test the success of Michelangelo's statue of Christ by searching out these various elements in it. We must also know what incident the artist had in mind of which the work is an illustration, so to speak.

The statue is called in Italian Cristo Risorto, that is, Christ Risen or Triumphant, because the reference is to a circumstance not recorded of his earthly career, but belonging to the time following his resurrection. It is connected with a story told by St. Ambrose about the apostle Peter. St. Peter, it is believed, spent the latter part of his life in Rome, where the cruel emperor, Nero, was doing his best to exterminate the Christians.

"After the burning of Rome, Nero threw upon the Christians the accusation of having fired the city. This was the origin of the first persecution, in which many perished by terrible and hitherto unheard-of deaths. The Christian converts besought Peter not to expose his life, which was dear and necessary to the well-being of all; and at length he consented to depart from Rome. But as he fled along the Appian Way, about two miles from the gates, he was met by a vision of our Saviour, travelling towards the city. Struck with amazement, he exclaimed, 'Lord! whither goest thou?' (Domine, quo vadis?) to which the Saviour, looking upon him with a mild sadness, replied, 'I go to Rome to be crucified a second time,' and vanished.

*Peter, [41] taking this for a sign that he was to submit himself to the suffer-
ings prepared for him, immediately turned back, and re-entered the city."*
[17]

[17] *From Mrs. Jameson's Sacred and Legendary Art, pages 200, 201.*

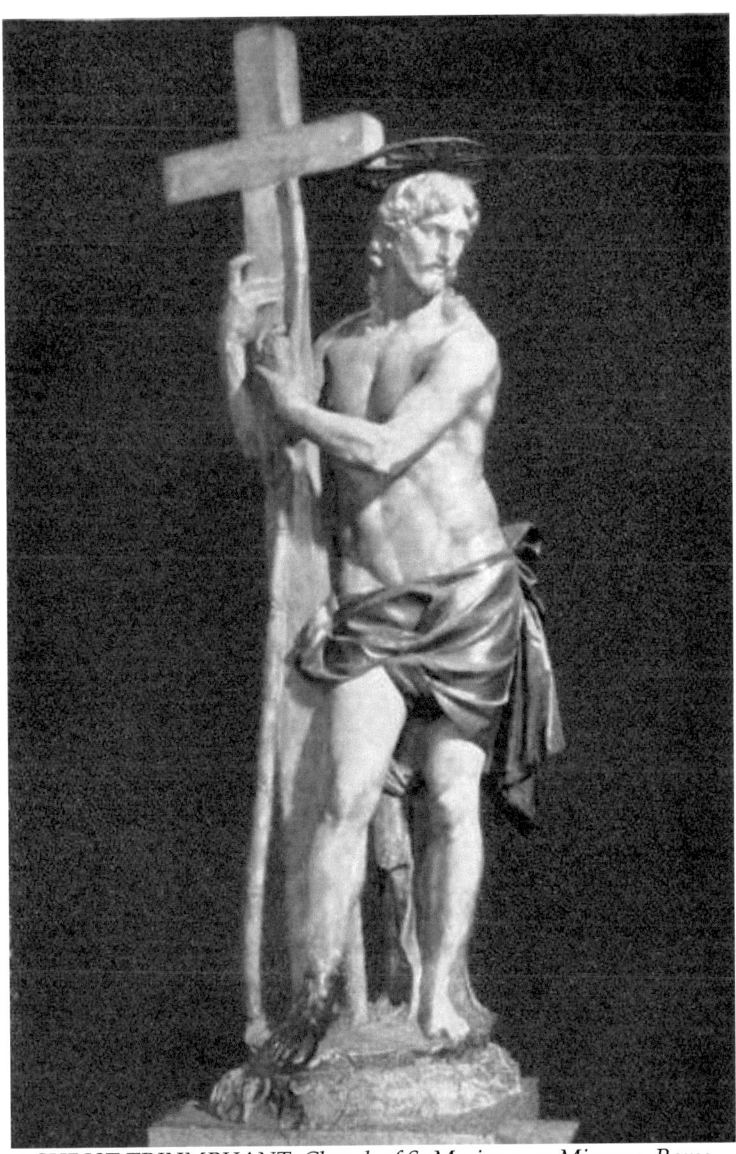

CHRIST TRIUMPHANT. Church of S. Maria sopra Minerva, Rome.

It is this visionary figure of the Christ, appearing and disappearing before the eyes of Peter, that Michelangelo represents in the statue. He carries a cross not large enough for an actual crucifixion, as that would be out of place here, but tall enough to show its real purpose. He has also the long reed and the sponge which the soldier used to give him a drink of vinegar and gall when he thirsted on the cross. A bit of rope is a reminder of the scourging given him by the governor.

All these things he carries with him to Rome for a fresh martyrdom. It is as if in walking along the way he suddenly meets Peter, and, at the apostle's astonished question, he pauses, leaning a moment on the cross, as he turns gently to reply.

Now as this is the Christ risen, or triumphant, the Christ who has conquered death and the grave, Michelangelo wanted to do all he could to make a noble-looking figure. The face is of the handsome type, with regular features, which the Italians like to give to their ideal of Christ. The expression of reproach is so gentle that one deserving rebuke may well feel ashamed before it.

The sorrow in the face is such as Jesus might have shown as he turned to Judas at the Last Supper. The gentleness in it is of the quality so attractive to children. There is, too, something of the [42] sympathetic element in it which Mary and Martha found.

The countenance is not without intellectuality, though it scarcely shows the keenness which the lawyers found it hard to outwit. It has rather the refinement of a lover of all that is beautiful. Nor is there much in expression or attitude to suggest the more commanding qualities of Jesus. These stronger elements the statue seems to lack.

It is rather puzzling to one who is trying to form standards of taste to learn that critics are divided in their opinion about this statue. It is, therefore, well to know that Michelangelo is not wholly responsible for the work as we now see it. Though he designed and began it, he left it to some unskilful apprentices to finish. The effect of the lines is injured by the bronze drapery which was added later. A bronze sandal has also been put on the right foot to protect it, as it had become much worn by kisses.

In criticising a statue one must always remember that it is best seen in the surroundings for which it is designed. It is said, even by one who does not greatly admire Michelangelo's Christ, that in the dim light of the church where it stands, "it diffuses a grace and sweetness which no repro-duction renders." [18]

[18] Symonds, in Life of Michelangelo Buonarotti.

[43]

VIII

THE CREATION OF MAN

Science has long been trying to solve the problem of the origin of the human race. Great books are published by learned men to explain how the being called man came to be what he is. But centuries before the beginnings of science a wonderful poem was written on the same subject of the crea-tion. This poem is called Genesis, that is, the Birth or Origin of things, and it forms a part of the first book of our Bible. Ever since it was written it has been one of the sacred books of many people.

This story of creation was once the favorite subject of artists. In the peri-od before the invention of printing, people depended for their instruction upon pictures about as much as we now do upon books. Painters some-times covered the walls and ceiling of churches with illustrations of the book of Genesis, transforming them into huge picture-books, from which the worshippers could learn the Bible stories which they were unable to read in books.

Michelangelo was one of the last Italian painters to do this, and he prof-ited by all the work that had been done before to make the grandest series of Genesis illustrations ever produced. It is from this [44] series that our illustration is taken, representing the subject of the Creation of Man. The painter did not try to follow the text very literally. In the book of Genesis we read: [19] —

[19] Genesis, chapter i verses 26-27; chapter ii verse 7.

"And God said, Let us make man in our image, after our likeness: and let them have dominion over the fish of the sea, and over the fowl of the air, and over the cattle, and over all the earth, and over every creeping thing that creepeth upon the earth.

"So God created man in his own image, in the image of God created he him.... And the Lord God formed man of the dust of the ground, and breathed into his nostrils the breath of life; and man became a living soul."

Michelangelo takes these words, and expresses, in his own way, the supreme creative moment when "man became a living soul."

The man Adam lies on a jutting promontory of the newly made land. Though his body is formed, he lacks as yet the inner force to use it; he is not yet alive. The Creator is borne along on a swirling cloud of cherubs, moving forward through space like a rushing mighty wind. Perhaps the painter was thinking of the psalmist's beautiful description of God's coming: [20] "He rode upon a cherub, and did fly: yea, he did fly upon the wings of the wind."

[20] Psalm xviii, verse 10.

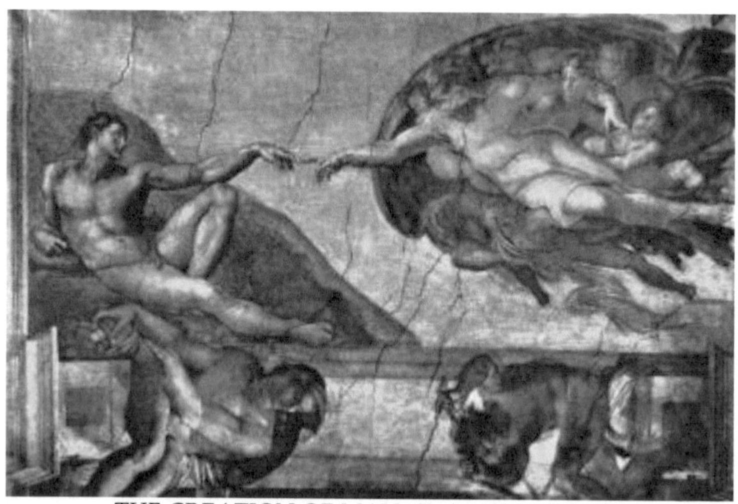

THE CREATION OF MAN. Sistine Chapel, Rome.

Please click here for a modern color image

In His fatherly face is expressed the good purpose to create a son "in his own image." The [47] cherubic host accompanying him are full of joy and awe. We are reminded of that time of which the poet Milton wrote, [21] when

> *"All*
> *The multitude of angels, with a shout*

Loud as from numbers without number, sweet
As from blest voices, uttering joy, — Heaven rung
With jubilee, and loud hosannas filled
The eternal regions."

[21] Paradise Lost, book iii. lines 344-349.

The sign of the Almighty's creative power is the outstretched arm extended towards Adam with a superb gesture of command. As if in answer to the divine summons, the lifeless figure begins to stir, rising slowly to a sitting posture. The face turns towards the source of life as the flower turns to the sun. The eyes are lifted to the Creator's with a wistful yearning. It is the look we sometimes see in the eyes of a woodland creature appealing for mercy. It is such a look as might belong to that imaginary being of the Greek mythology, the faun, half beast, half human. Thus Adam, still but half created, begins to feel the thrill of life in his members, and is aroused to action. He lifts his hand to meet the Creator's outstretched finger. The current of life is established, the vital spark is communicated, and in another moment Adam will rise in his full dignity as a human soul.

This picture was painted long before there was any knowledge of electricity, of electric sparks, and electric currents. Yet, if we did not know otherwise, we might fancy that Michelangelo had some [48] of these wonderful ideas of modern science in mind, as the symbols of the great thoughts he was trying to express.

The picture suggests to our latter day scientific imagination that God's currents of power move as silently, as swiftly, as invisibly and mysteriously as the currents of electricity. The painter meant to show that the work of creation was not a mechanical effort of the Almighty, but that with him a gesture, a word, even a thought, brings something into being.

The series of which this picture forms a part is painted in fresco on the ceiling of the Sistine Chapel, in the Pope's palace of the Vatican, Rome. To break up the monotony of the long plain surface he had to decorate, the painter divided the strip of space in the centre into nine compartments. These are separated from each other by a painted architectural framework, so cunningly represented that it seems to project from the ceiling like a solid structure of beams.

Our illustration shows a portion of the simulated framework which incloses the picture. On what appears to be a pedestal at each corner is a seated figure representing a statue. One is a beautiful youth with a horn of plenty, and the other is a faun-like creature capering gayly. The purpose of these figures is decorative, like those in the background of the Holy Family.

[49]

IX

JEREMIAH

Michelangelo's decoration of the Sistine Chapel ceiling did not stop with the series of panels running along the flat space in the centre. On either side, where the ceiling arches to meet the side walls, he painted a row of figures, which seem to be seated in sculptured niches. There are twelve of these figures in all, and seven of them are Hebrew prophets.

The prophets were holy men of old, who walked with God, and carried his messages among men. They were men of great courage and conviction, fearlessly denouncing the sins of their times. Sometimes they were great reformers, bringing about by their preaching an improved condition of things. Often their mission was to arouse hope in discouragement, to strengthen faith in a happier time to come. They looked forward to a future day, when the Prince of Peace should reign in the earth.

Jeremiah was a prophet of Judah during the corrupt and troublous times in the reigns of Josiah, Jehoiakim, and Zedekiah. He has been compared by a recent writer [22] to "a Puritan living in the age of the Stuarts, to a Huguenot living in the age of [50] the Medici, or a Savonarola living in the age of Pope Alexander VI." He was born in Anathoth, a little village of Judæa and being the son of a priest was consecrated to the priesthood from birth.

[22] Lyman Abbott in Hebrew Prophets and American Problems.

He was still very young when it was borne in upon him that to be loyal to God he must stand forth and speak the truth more boldly than other priests were doing. Shrinking from such a task, he besought God to spare him. "Ah, Lord God! behold, I cannot speak: for I am a child."

70

And this, writes Jeremiah, is the answer he received: [23] *"Say not, I am a child: for thou shalt go to all that I shall send thee, and whatsoever I command thee thou shalt speak. Be not afraid of their faces: for I am with thee to deliver thee, saith the Lord. Then the Lord put forth his hand, and touched my mouth. And the Lord said unto me, Behold, I have put my words in thy mouth. See, I have this day set thee over the nations and over the kingdoms, to root out, and to pull down, and to destroy, and to throw down, to build, and to plant."*

[23] *Jeremiah, chapter i. verses 6-10.*

Thus Jeremiah became a prophet, and from that time on his life was "one long, hopeless protest against folly and crime." Earnestly he besought his people to return to God before it was too late: "O Jerusalem, wash thine heart from wickedness, that thou mayest be saved;" [24] *but prayers and threats were alike of no avail, and misfortunes began to afflict the land. Then Jeremiah shows himself a true patriot. Though his people refused to hear him, he still loves them and pleads their cause. In the horror of famine, he prays to God in their behalf.*

[24] *Ibid., ch. iv. v. 14.*

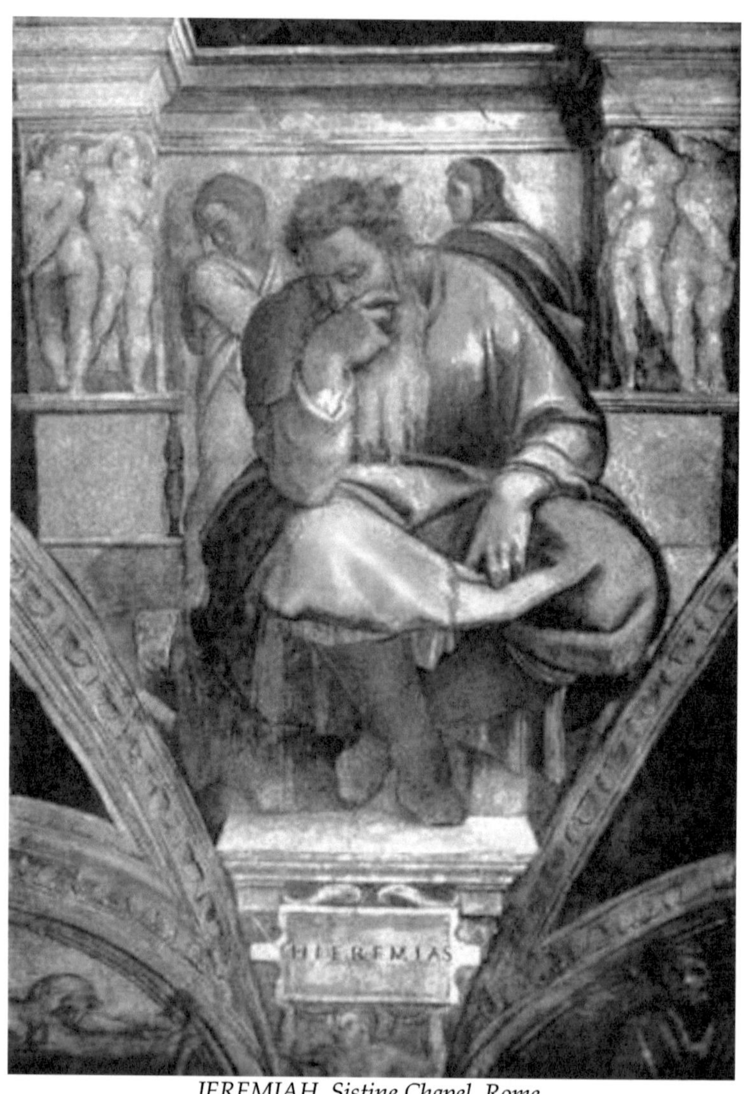

JEREMIAH. Sistine Chapel, Rome.

[53]

Please click here for a modern color image

There are times even in the midst of disappointment when Jeremiah has some gleam of hope for the future. He predicts the days when "a King shall reign and prosper, and shall execute judgment and justice in the earth." [25] Such times he himself was never to enjoy. He lived to see the Babylonian invasion, Jerusalem besieged and laid waste, and his people taken captive. The reward of his faithful warnings was to be cast into prison by the ungrateful King Zedekiah. Finally he was carried by the remnant of his people into Egypt, where he died in a sad and lonely old age.

[25] Jeremiah, chapter xxiii. verse 5.

Once in a moment of discouragement early in life, his grief had burst forth in words which might well express the feelings of his old age: "Oh that my head were waters, and mine eyes a fountain of tears, that I might weep day and night for the slain of the daughter of my people!" [26]

[26] Jeremiah, chapter ix. verse 1.

All the pathos of these words is conveyed in Michelangelo's wonderful figure of Jeremiah. The story of his life is written in his face and attitude. He is an old man, with long gray beard, but he still has the splendid vigor which comes from plain and simple living. He sits with bowed head, lost in thought, his long life passing in review before his [54] mind's eye. His message is spoken, his race is run; he is weary of life and longs to die. There is something inexpressibly moving in his profound melancholy.

The painter has placed just behind the prophet two little figures which are like attendant spirits. They seem to sympathize with Jeremiah's sorrows. The figures ornamenting the sculptured niche remind us of those in the background of the Holy Family and have a similar decorative purpose.

Those who have studied the history of the times in which Michelangelo lived may find in this figure of Jeremiah an expression of the artist's own character. Like the old Hebrew prophet, he lived in the midst of a corruption which he was helpless to remedy, and which saddened his inmost soul. His own life was full of disappointments. In his lonely old age he wrote a sonnet, which is not unlike some of Jeremiah's utterances, and which is a clue to the meaning of the picture: —

> *"Borne to the utmost brink of life's dark sea,*
> *Too late thy joys I understand, O earth!*
> *How thou dost promise peace which cannot be,*

And that repose which ever dies at birth.
The retrospect of life through many a day,
Now to its close attained by Heaven's decree,
Brings forth from memory, in sad array,
Only old errors, fain forgot by me, —
Errors which e'en, if long life's erring day,
To soul destruction would have led my way.
For this I know — the greatest bliss on high
Belongs to him called earliest to die."

[55]

X

DANIEL

In striking contrast to the bowed and sorrowful old prophet Jeremiah is the alert and eager youth Daniel. The two men were contemporaries, though there was a difference in their ages. When, in the reign of Jehoiakim, the Jews were taken into captivity to Babylon, the youth Daniel went with them, while the old prophet Jeremiah was left behind. Daniel was chosen, with three companions, to be educated at the court of the Babylonian king, Nebuchadnezzar. They were taught the Chaldean language and the sciences, and the king was delighted with their progress.

An opportunity soon came for Daniel to be of service to his royal patron. Nebuchadnezzar had a strange dream, which none of his magicians could interpret, because, unfortunately, he had forgotten it. In his anger that no one could supply the lost memory, he commanded to destroy all the wise men of Babylon. But Daniel prayed to God that the secret might be revealed to him.

His prayers were answered, and he related to the king not only just what the dream was, but the full meaning of it: [27] "Thou, O king, sawest, and behold [56] a great image. This great image, whose brightness was excellent, stood before thee; and the form thereof was terrible. This image's head was of fine gold, his breast and his arms of silver, his belly and his thighs of *brass, his legs of iron, his feet part of iron and part of clay. Thou sawest till that a stone was cut out without hands, which smote the image upon his feet that were of iron and clay, and brake them to pieces.... And the stone that smote the image became a great mountain, and filled the whole earth."*

[27] Daniel, chapter ii. verses 31-35.

In Daniel's interpretation the different portions of the image represented the different kingdoms which should follow, one after another, in the future. The stone which brake the image in pieces referred to the final kingdom which the God of heaven shall set up, "which shall never be destroyed," but which shall stand forever.

From this time forth Daniel became a seer. He had many wonderful visions in the night, and interpreted them with reference to future historical events. He was also a statesman, the king having made him governor of the province as a reward for his services. In later years he acted as viceroy at a time when the king was insane.

In the reign of Nebuchadnezzar's successor, Belshazzar, Daniel was again called into service as a seer. One night, during a great feast, a mysterious hand appeared to write some inscription on the wall, and Daniel alone could interpret it. The message was ominous, but the prophet spoke out boldly. [59] "Mene, Mene, Tekel, Upharsin," ran the words, "Thou art weighed in the balances and art found wanting." Daniel condemned the king for his iniquities, and declared that his kingdom should be divided by the Medes and Persians. That very night Belshazzar was slain, and Darius, the Median, took the kingdom.

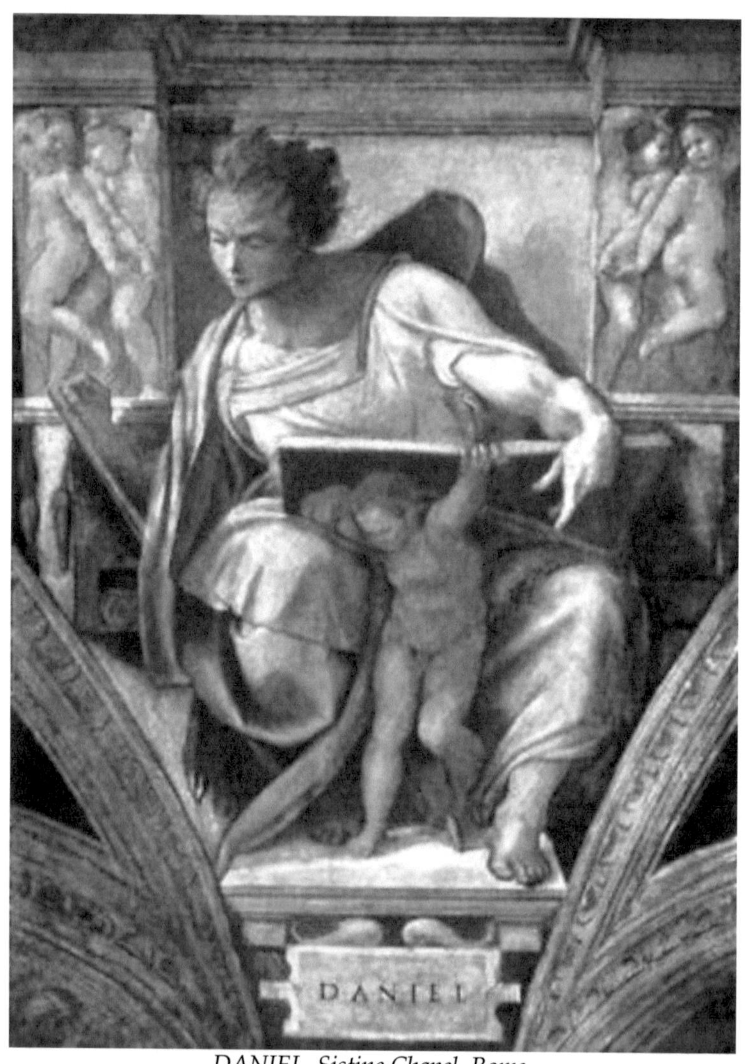

DANIEL. Sistine Chapel, Rome.

Please click here for a modern color image

Under the new dynasty Daniel was given so much power that some of the officials, jealous of his preferment, plotted against him. They contrived to persuade King Darius to sign a decree that "whosoever should ask a petition of any god or man for thirty days, save of the king himself, should be cast into the den of lions." The officials were right in supposing that this would entrap Daniel into law-breaking, for, faithful to his Hebrew training, he offered prayer to God three times a day. He was therefore cast into the lions' den, but no harm befell him, because, according to his own explanation, God sent his angel to shut the lions' mouths.

Daniel continued to hold office even in the reign of the next king, Cyrus the Persian. He lived to a great old age, but he was so young when he first showed his prophetic gifts that it is natural to think of him in his youth as Michelangelo has represented him. It would seem that the artist had in mind Daniel's early years of education at court. On his lap is a large open book supported on the back of a tiny figure standing between his knees. This may represent a volume of Chaldean learning. His posture shows that he has been consulting the volume, [60] and now turns to his writing tablets to record his own thoughts.

His broad forehead shows him to be a student and a thinker. The waving hair is brushed back to form an aureole about his face. It is the face of a dreamer in a moment of inspiration. Eagerly he writes his words of mingled poetry and prophecy. He is full of youthful enthusiasm for his work, a nature fitted for action as well as for vision. He has also the spirited bearing of one who fears neither the rage of a lion nor the wrath of a king. There is a breezy energy in his motions, as if thoughts came more swiftly than he could transcribe them.

His expression of happy anticipation is in vivid contrast to Jeremiah's sorrowful attitude of retrospection. The picture brings out clearly the fact that the keynote of Daniel's prophecy is hope. Looking into his rapt face, we may imagine that this is the message he is writing: "They that be wise shall shine as the brightness of the firmament; and they that turn many to righteousness, as the stars forever and ever." [28]

[28] Daniel, chapter xii. verse 3.

[61]

XI

THE DELPHIC SIBYL

In the rows of figures which Michelangelo painted along the arched portion of the ceiling of the Sistine Chapel, the prophets are associated with sibyls. Hence, in the plan of decoration, there comes first the figure of a man, and then the figure of a woman.

Now, as the Bible contains no allusion to sibyls, it may seem strange that they should have a place in a series of Bible illustrations, and especially that they should appear side by side with the prophets. To explain this, we must learn something about the sibyls.

They were women of ancient times supposed to have supernatural gifts of foretelling the future. They devoted themselves to solitude and meditation, and sometimes lived apart in caves or grottoes. Sometimes they were connected with temples, and delivered what were supposed to be the messages of the gods to the worshippers. These messages were called oracles, and were greatly revered by the people who consulted the gods.

Some of the sibyls' words of wisdom were committed to writing and passed down to following generations. Though they lived in heathen coun [62] tries, the tradition ran that they prophesied the advent of Christ. There is a passage in one of Virgil's eclogues (the fourth) upon which the supposition is based. Early in the Christian era, when men were spreading the new faith, they made much of these sibylline prophecies to add weight to their teachings.

In former times, fact and fable were very often confused, and people did not take pains to distinguish the legends of the sibyls from the history of the prophets. When the Latin hymn "Dies Irae" was written, the sibyl was mentioned, with the prophet, as predicting the final destruction of the world. Many painters and sculptors gave the two equal honor in the same way. In the prevailing opinion, the sibyls shared with the prophets an inspired foreknowledge of the Christian faith.

The nine main panels of Michelangelo's ceiling decoration show how man was created, and how he was tempted and fell into sin. To carry on still further the story of the human race, the painter shows the succession of men and women, prophets and sibyls, who, one after another, predicted the redemption of the world in Christ. On the side walls, below these figures, the story is carried to completion in a series of pictures illustrating the life of Christ. The last named frescoes were painted by various artists some years before Michelangelo's work on the ceiling.

The number of sibyls was given as ten or twelve, and of these Michelangelo selected five. His idea [65] here, as with the prophets, seemed to be to represent some in old age and some in youth.

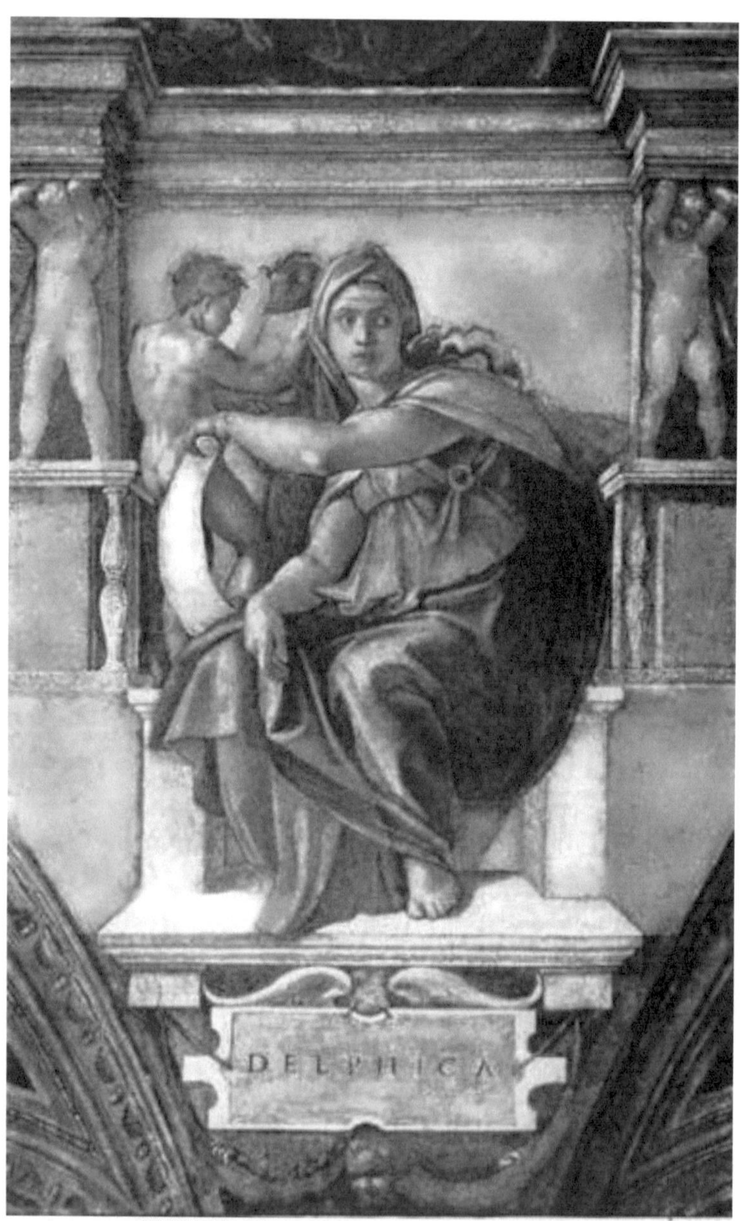

THE DELPHIC SIBYL. Sistine Chapel, Rome.

Please click here for a modern color image

The Delphic sibyl is the youngest and most beautiful of them all. She presided over the temple of Apollo in the Greek town of Delphi, where it was long customary for the priestess, or pythia, as she was called, to be a young woman selected from some family of poor country people.

The temple at Delphi was one of great celebrity. In the centre was a small opening in the ground, whence arose an intoxicating vapor, and over this sat the pythia, on a three-legged seat, or tripod, and delivered the oracle communicated to her by the god. These oracles were delivered in verse.

The Delphic sibyl, or pythia, of Michelangelo's picture, has the splendid stature of an Amazon. Her head is draped with a sort of Greek turban, beneath which her hair escapes in flying curls. Her face and expression show her at once to be unlike an ordinary woman. She has the look of a startled fawn, which has suddenly heard the call of a distant voice. She turns her head in the attitude of one listening. She looks far away with eyes that see visions, but what those visions are none can guess. There are other pictures of the same sibyl carrying a crown of thorns, showing that she predicted the sufferings of Christ. Perhaps this is the meaning of the sorrowful expression in these wide eyes.

The scroll which she unrolls in her left hand is the scroll of her prophecy. The two little figures holding a book, just behind her right shoulder, are [66] genii, or spirits, symbolic of her inspiration. One reads eagerly from the volume while the other listens with rapt attention.

The picture makes a very interesting study in the composition of lines. Starting from the topmost point of the turban, draw a line on the right, coming across the shoulder along the outer edge of the drapery to the toe. On the left, let the line connecting the same two points follow the outer curve of the scroll, along the slanting edge of the mantle, and we get a beautiful pointed oval as the basis of the composition.

The sibyl's left arm drops a curve across the upper part of the figure, and this curve is repeated a little lower down by the creases in the drapery across the lap. Such are the few strong, simple lines which compose the picture, producing an effect of grandeur which a confusion of many lines would entirely spoil.

[67]

XII

THE CUMBN SIBYL

Of all the sibyls, the one we hear most about is the Cum栢. The legend runs that, having asked a boon of Apollo, she gathered a handful of sand and said, "Grant me to see as many birthdays as there are sand grains in my hand." The wish was gratified, but unluckily she forgot to ask for enduring youth, so she was doomed to live a thousand years in a withered old age. Thus we always think of her as an old woman, as Michelangelo has represented her.

She is called the Cum栢 sibyl because she is supposed to have lived in Cum夊which was the oldest and one of the most important of the Greek colonies in Italy. Her real name, we are told, was Demos. She lived in a great cavern, where the people came to consult her, and her answers to their questions were regarded as oracles, or answers from the deities. She used to write on the leaves of trees the names and fates of different persons, arranging them in her cave to be read by her votaries. Sometimes the wind sweeping through the cavern scattered the leaves broadcast through the world.

The manner of consulting her is fully described by the Latin poet Virgil in the sixth book of the [68] Teid. He tells how Teas, arriving with his fellow voyagers at the town of Cum夊immediately goes to the temple of Apollo,

> *"And seeks the cave of wondrous size,*
> *The sibyl's dread retreat,*
> *The sibyl, whom the Delian seer*
> *Inspires to see the future clear,*
> *And fills with frenzy's heat;*
> *The grove they enter, and behold*
> *Above their heads the roof of gold.*
>
> *"Within the mountain's hollow side,*
> *A cavern stretches high and wide;*
> *A hundred entries thither lead;*
> *A hundred voices thence proceed,*

Each uttering forth the sibyl's rede.
The sacred threshold now they trod:
'Pray for an answer! pray! the god,'
She cries, 'the god is nigh!'

"And as before the door in view
She stands, her visage pales its hue,
Her locks dishevelled fly,
Her breath comes thick, her wild heart glows.
Dilating as the madness grows,
Her form looks larger to the eye;
Unearthly peals her deep-toned cry,
As, breathing nearer and more near,
The god comes rushing on his seer."

Teas now begs a favor of the sibyl. He has heard that here the path leads downward to the dead, and he desires to go thither to visit his father, Anchises. There are certain conditions to fulfil before setting forth, but when these are done the sibyl guides him on his way, and the journey is safely made.

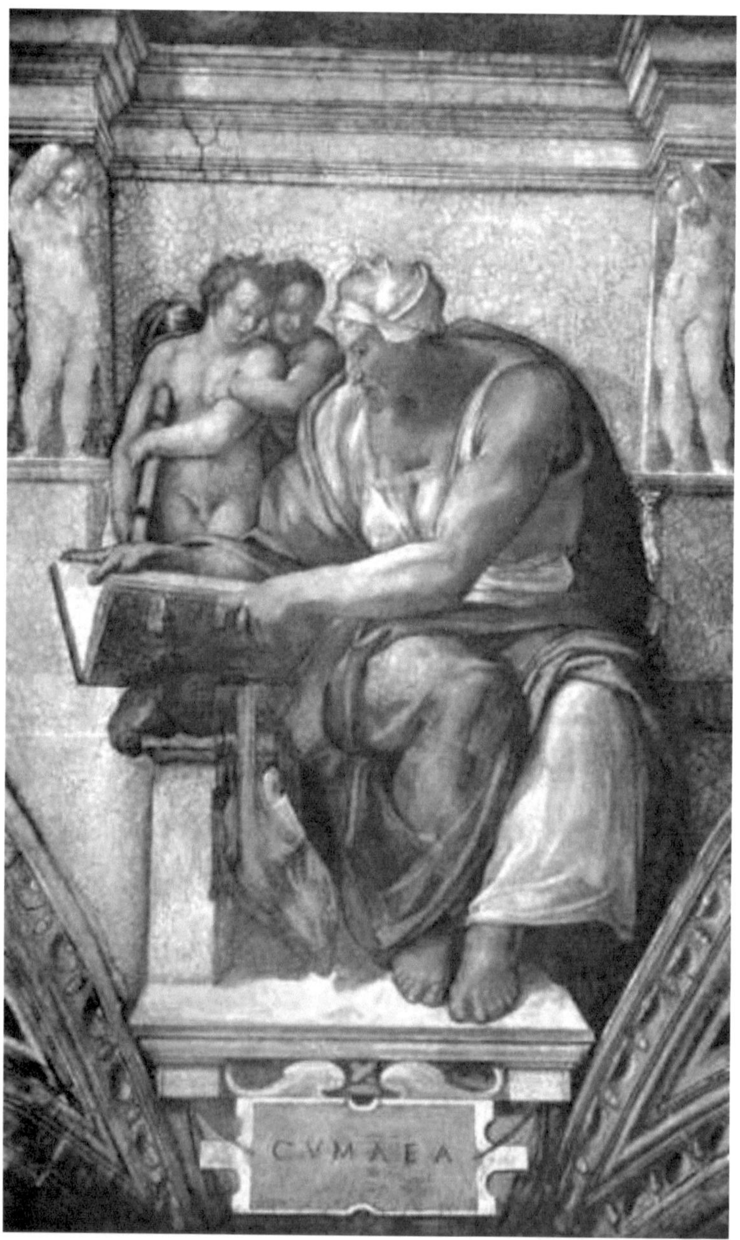

CVMAEA

[71]

Please click here for a modern color image

Another legend of the Cum柘 sibyl has to do with the Roman emperor Tarquin. The sibyl came to him one day with nine books of oracles, which she wished him to buy. The price was exorbitant, and the emperor refused her demand. She then went away, burned three of the books, and, returning with the remaining six, made the same demand. Again her offer was refused, and again she burned three books and returned, still requiring the original price for the three that were left. Tarquin now consulted the soothsayers, and, acting upon their advice, bought the books, which were found to contain directions concerning the religion and policy of Rome.

For many years they were held sacred, and were carefully preserved in the temple of Jupiter in the Capitol, under the care of official guardians. At length the temple was destroyed by fire, and the original sibylline books perished. In the following centuries they were replaced by scattered papers, collected from time to time in various parts of the empire, purporting to be the writings of the sibyl. These sibylline leaves, as they were called, contained passages supposed to be prophetic of the coming of Christ, and this is why the Cum柘 sibyl is placed by Michelangelo among the prophets.

The sibyl is reading aloud from one of her books of oracles. The two little genii standing behind her shoulder, and listening with absorbed attention, hold another book, not yet unclusped, ready for her. She reads her prophecy with keen, searching eyes, [72] and a manner that is almost stern. We can see in the large, strong features the determination of her character.

It is not a gentle face, and not pleasing, but it is full of meaning. We read there the record of the centuries which have passed over her head, bringing her the deep secrets of life. Yet the prophecies are still unfulfilled, and there is a look of unsatisfied longing in her wrinkled old face.

You will notice that the outlines of the Cum柘 sibyl are drawn in an oval figure similar to that inclosing the Delphic sibyl. Here, however, the oval is of a more elongated form, and the left side is broken midway by the introduction of the book.

The old writer Pausanias, writing his "Description of Greece," in the second century, says that the people of Cum柘howed a small stone urn in the temple of Apollo containing the ashes of the sibyl. For many centuries her cavern was pointed out to travellers in a rock under the citadel of Cum殑Finally the fortifications of the city were undermined, but to this day a subterranean passage in the rock on which they were built is still shown as the entrance to the sibyl's cave.

[73]

XIII

LORENZO DE' MEDICI

The statue of Lorenzo de' Medici is the central figure on the tomb erected to the memory of this prince. He was the rather unworthy namesake of his illustrious grandfather, who was known as Lorenzo the Magnificent. The Medici family was for many generations the richest and most powerful in Florence. They were originally merchants, and, as the name signifies, physicians, and, accumulating great wealth, they became powerful leaders, and really the rulers of the republic.

Some of them were munificent patrons of art and literature. There was one named Cosimo, who did so much to make his city famous that he was called Pater Patriae, the father of the country, as was, centuries afterwards, our own Washington. His grandson Lorenzo won the title of the Magnificent for his lavish generosity and superb plans for the advancement of art and learning. So much power could not safely be in the hands of a single family. The Medici, from being benefactors, finally became tyrants.

The Lorenzo of this statue was one of the more insignificant members of the family. It is said that "he inherited the vices without the genius of the [74] family, and was ambitious, unscrupulous, and dissipated. His uncle, Pope Leo X., after depriving the Duke of Urbino of his hereditary domains, bestowed them, with the title of duke, on Lorenzo, whom he also made general of the pontifical forces." [29] In 1518 Leo united him in marriage to a French princess, and their daughter was the afterwards celebrated Catharine de' Medici, queen of the French king, Henry II. These are the main facts in the life of a man who is remembered only because he had illustrious ancestors, a famous daughter, and a superb tomb.

[29] Susan and Joanna Horner's Walks in Florence, vol. i. p. 125.

It mattered nothing to Michelangelo that he had so poor a subject for a statue. It is supposed that he made no attempt at correct portraiture in the figure. The insignificant Lorenzo was transformed by the magic of his genius into a hero.

He wears a suit of Roman armor, in accordance with his career as a general in the wars with the Duke of Urbino, whose title he took. His helmet is pulled well forward over the brow, the head is bent, the cheek rests upon the left hand, the elbow supported on a casket placed on the knee. With finger laid thoughtfully upon the lips, he is thinking intently. The right hand rests, palm out, against the knee in a characteristic position of inaction.

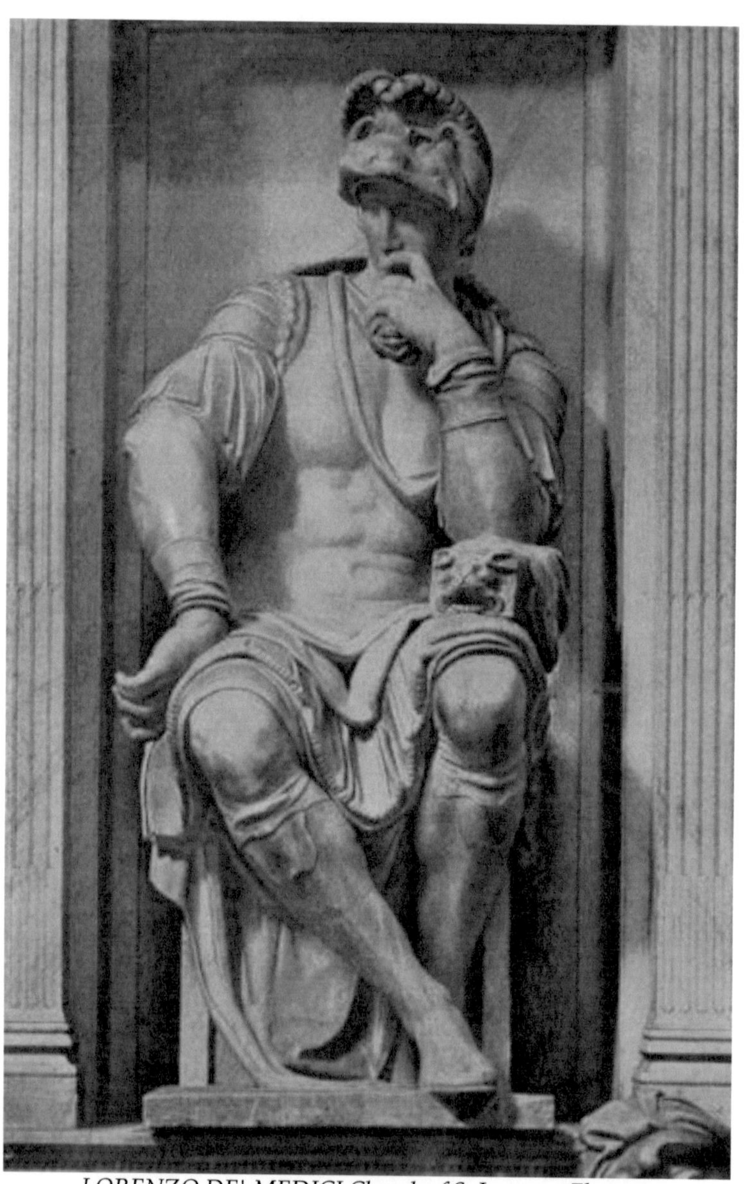

LORENZO DE' MEDICI Church of S. Lorenzo, Florence

His mood is not that of a dreamer lost to his present surroundings. Rather he seems to be keenly aware of what is going on; his meditations have to do with the present. It is as if, having given an order, he awaits its execution, his mind still intent [77] upon his purposes, satisfied with his decision, and calmly expectant of its success. His affair is one of serious importance; no trifling matter absorbs the thought of this grave man. "A king sits in this attitude when, in the midst of his army, he orders the execution of some judicial act, like the destruction of a city. Frederic Barbarossa must have appeared thus when he caused Milan to be ploughed up." [30]

[30] Taine, Travels in Italy.

The lack of resemblance in the statue to the original duke Lorenzo made it for a long time doubtful whether it was intended to be his tomb. The Florentines, in their poetic way, fell into the habit of calling it Il Pensiero, that is, Thought, or Meditation, sometimes Il Pensieroso, The Thinker. These are, after all, the best names for the statue, which is allegorical rather than historical in its intention. The great English poet Milton has written a poem, which is like a companion piece to the statue, fitting it as words sometimes fit music. It begins in this way, in words which Il Pensieroso himself might speak: —

> *"Hence, vain deluding Joys,*
> *The brood of Folly, without father bred!*
> *How little you bested,*
> *Or fill the fix構mind with all your toys!*
> *Dwell in some idle brain,*
> *And fancies fond with gaudy shape possess,*
> *As thick and numberless*
> *As the gay motes that people the sunbeams,*
> *Or likest hovering dreams,*
> *The fickle pensioners of Morpheus' train.*
> *But hail! thou Goddess sage and holy,*
> *Hail, divinest Melancholy!"*

[78] Lorenzo's statue stands in a niche above the sarcophagus, or stone coffin, in which his body was laid. On the top of the sarcophagus are two reclining figures called Dawn and Twilight. The tomb itself is in a chapel,

or sacristy, called the New Sacristy (to distinguish it from one still older), in the Church of S. Lorenzo, Florence. The entire sacristy is devoted to the memory of the Medici family, who had for several generations been benefactors of this church.

Now Michelangelo had a great deal to do with this family first and last, and his work on the tomb has an additional interest on this account. It was to Lorenzo the Magnificent that he owed his first start as a sculptor in an academy founded by this prince. He so pleased his patron that he was received into the duke's own household, and treated almost like a son. Years passed; Lorenzo had long been dead, when, one after another, two members of the same family came to the papal throne, and they desired to honor their name by employing the greatest sculptor of Italy in this monumental work.

So Michelangelo began designs for the sacristy, the entire decoration of which was intrusted to him. The walls of the rooms were panelled with marble, set with niches, in the form of windows, in which the statues were to be placed.

As the work proceeded, it was interrupted by some strange incidents, of which we shall hear later. The whole plan was never fully carried out, but in spite of incompleteness the chapel is a grand and impressive place.

[79]

XIV

THE TOMB OF GIULIANO DE' MEDICI

The tomb of Giuliano de' Medici is the companion to the tomb of Lorenzo, and stands on the opposite side of the altar which separates them. Our illustration shows the entire work, the statue being in the niche above, and the sarcophagus standing below with two reclining figures on it.

Giuliano de' Medici, duke of Nemours, was the youngest son of Lorenzo the Magnificent, and consequently the uncle of the younger Lorenzo. In reality he was greatly superior to his nephew, but curiously enough his appearance in Michelangelo's statue is more commonplace, though his attitude is graceful. He was a thoughtful man, somewhat melancholy in disposition, and the author of a poem on suicide. He wears the costume of a

Roman general, but his small head and slender throat are not those of a warrior.

You will notice that the attitude of the duke Giuliano is somewhat similar to that of Moses. Both sit with left foot drawn back and right knee extended. Both turn the head in profile, looking intently toward the left. In either case it is easy to imagine the figure suddenly springing up.

Now this fact emphasizes the difference we have [80] already noted between the sculpture of Michelangelo and that of the Greeks. The leading idea in Greek sculpture was that of repose, while, as we have seen in the David and the Cupid, Michelangelo chose for his figures a moment of action. To give this suggestion of motion to a seated figure is even more remarkable than in the case of one standing, for the sitting posture naturally has an effect of stability.

The reclining figures on the sarcophagus of the Duke Giuliano represent Night and Day, and are supposed to be symbolic of death and resurrection. Night is a woman lying with head sunk upon the breast in a deep sleep. She is crowned with a crescent moon and star, and an owl is placed at her feet. The mask beneath her pillow symbolizes the body from which the spirit has departed. Though the figure is not beautiful in the Greek sense, it is grand and queenly. Opposite is Day, an unfinished captive, his head half freed from the stone, the arms rigid, the body contorted.

These two figures, together with Dawn and Twilight on Lorenzo's tomb, have an allegorical meaning which must be read in the light of Michelangelo's own life history. "Life is a dream between two slumbers; sleep is death's twin-brother; night is the shadow of death; death is the gate of life — such is the mysterious mythology wrought by the sculptor." [31]

[31] Symonds, in Renaissance in Italy: the Fine Arts.

The work on the Medicean tombs covered a period of about twelve years. During this time the Medici [83] family passed through varying fortunes, and in consequence the fate of the tombs, and indeed that of the sculptor himself, hung in the balance. Florence became weary of tyranny and rose in a revolution which drove the Medici from the city in 1527.

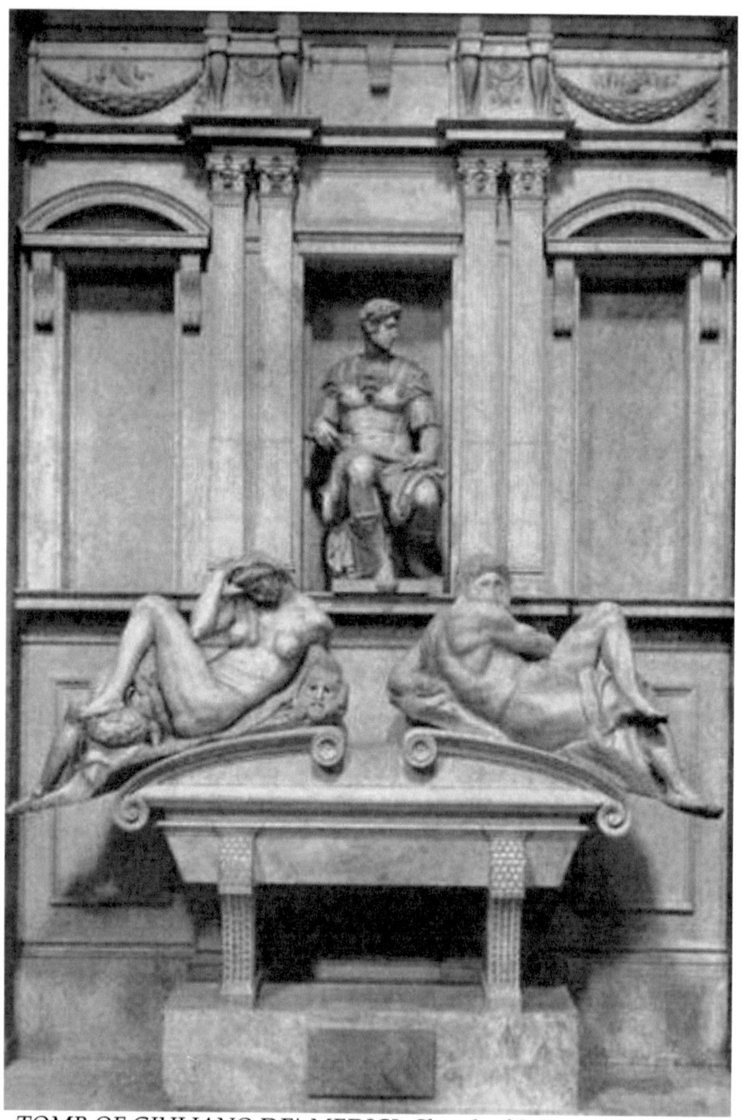

TOMB OF GIULIANO DE' MEDICI. Church of S. Lorenzo, Florence.

Success was of short duration: the republic soon "found herself standing out against a world of foes," the Pope, Clement VII. (himself a Medici), "threatening fire and flame," and all the Medici family *"getting ready to return in double force."* The Florentines prepared to fight for their liberty, and Michelangelo was found among the patriots. No sense of personal gratitude to the Medici could shake his love of liberty. He forsook the monuments and turned his skill to the fortification of the city.

For eleven months Florence was besieged, and in the end the city was captured. The Medici returned conquerors. Mercenaries now broke into the houses, killing the best citizens. Had not Michelangelo been in hiding, he too would have perished. But the Pope could not afford to lose his best sculptor, and, calling him forth from his hiding-place, again set him to work in the Medici chapel. It is not strange that the sculptor's proud spirit rebelled at having to work on that which was to honor the enemies of his beloved Florence.

Thus it was that his sculpture told the story of "the tragedy of Florence: how hope had departed, how life had become a desert, and how it was hard to struggle with waking consciousness, but good to [84] sleep and forget — nay, best of all, to be stone and feel no more."

The old writer Vasari, who was once a pupil of Michelangelo, and tells us many anecdotes of the sculptor, relates that when the statue of Night was first shown to the public, it called forth a verse from a contemporary poet (Giovan Battista Strozzi). This is the verse: —

> "Night in so sweet an attitude beheld
> Asleep, was by an angel sculptured
> In this stone; and sleeping, is alive;
> Waken her, doubter; she will speak to thee." [32]

To this Michelangelo replied in the following lines: [33] —

> "Welcome is sleep, more welcome sleep of stone
> Whilst crime and shame continue in the land;
> My happy fortune not to see or hear;
> Waken me not; — in mercy whisper low." [32]

The artist's verse may be taken as a keynote to the solemn tragedy of the work. In fact, the monuments are not really to Lorenzo and Giuliano, but to Florence, to "the great city which had struggled and erred so long, which had gone astray and repented, and suffered and erred again, but always mightily, with full tide of life in her veins and consciousness in her heart, until now the time had come when she was dead and past, chained down by icy oppression in a living grave." [34]

[32] Both translations are from Horners' Walks in Florence. Symonds has also translated the verses, but less literally.

[33] Swinburne in his lines, "In San Lorenzo," answers these lines, "Is thine hour come to waken, slumbering Night?"

[34] This and the preceding quotations are from Mrs. Oliphant's Makers of Florence.

[85]

XV

CENTRAL FIGURES IN THE LAST JUDGMENT

There are in the Bible certain references to a great day when the Son of Man shall be seen "coming in the clouds with great power and glory." "And he shall send his angels with a great sound of a trumpet, and they shall gather together his elect from the four winds, from one end of heaven to the other." [35] St. Paul, in a letter which he wrote to the Christians in Corinth, speaks of this as a "mystery," and says: [36] "We shall not all sleep, but we shall all be changed, in a moment, in the twinkling of an eye, at the last trump: for the trumpet shall sound, and the dead shall be raised incorruptible, and we shall be changed."

[35] Matthew, chapter xxiv. verse 31.

[36] 1 Corinthians, chapter xv. verses 51, 52.

In the Middle Ages these passages were interpreted very literally and had a great influence over the people. At that time the Christian religion was a religion of fear rather than of love, and men were continually picturing in their minds God's angry separation of the good from the wicked.

How much such thoughts occupied them we may see from Dante's great poem describing a vision of [86] the Inferno, Purgatory, and Paradise. This was written in the thirteenth century, and in the same period appeared a short Latin lyric, or hymn, called "Dies Irae," or the Day of Wrath, from an expression used by the old Hebrew prophet Zephaniah. The author was a Franciscan monk named Thomas of Celano, and we may see how deeply he felt from these verses: —

> *"Ah! what terror is impending*
> *When the Judge is seen descending,*
> *And each secret veil is rending.*

> *"To the throne, the trumpet sounding,*
> *Through the sepulchres resounding,*
> *Summons all, with voice astounding.*

> *"Sits the Judge, the raised arraigning,*
> *Darkest mysteries explaining,*
> *Nothing unavenged remaining."*

This vivid word picture forms the subject of many great paintings by the older Italian masters, known under the title of the Last Judgment. Michelangelo's was one of the last of these, and in general arrangement his composition resembles those of his predecessors.

From the upper air a company of angels descends, carrying a cross, a crown of thorns, and other instruments of the Saviour's sufferings. Below them is the Judge himself surrounded by the apostles and other saints. Underneath are the archangels blowing their trumpets. On earth, in the lowest part of the picture at the left, the dead rise from their graves and ascend through the air to the Judge. At the right, opposite the ascending dead, are the condemned sinners, descending to the boat which will carry them over the river Styx into the Inferno.

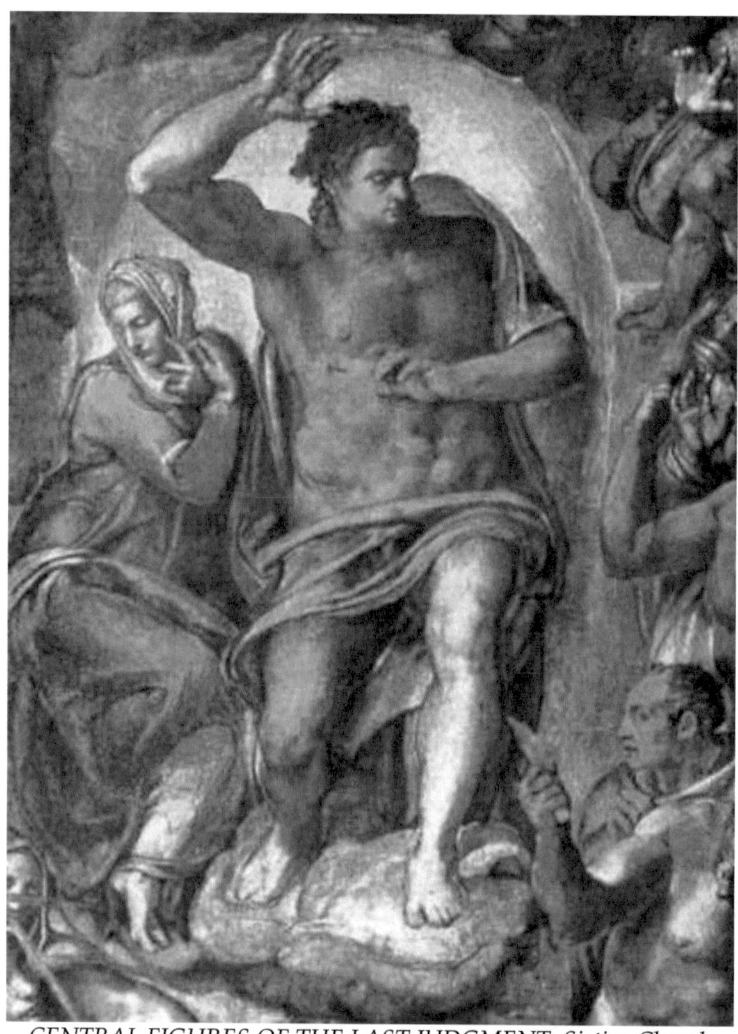

CENTRAL FIGURES OF THE LAST JUDGMENT. *Sistine Chapel, Rome.*

[89]

Please click here for a modern color image

Our illustration gives only the central figures in this great multitude, the Divine Judge accompanied by his mother. He is a man of mighty mus-

cular power, young and handsome, with an expression of imperious dignity. Enthroned on the clouds, he seems just rising from a sitting posture to
execute his judgments. He lifts his arms in a sweeping motion as if to part
the multitudes pressing upon him on both sides. In so doing he shows the
wound in his right side made by the soldier's spear at the crucifixion. Neither expression nor gesture manifests anger; those beautiful hands with
delicately extended fingers will strike no blow. The gesture itself is a command.

Beneath Christ's upraised arm, on his right side, sits his Mother Mary.
Each must interpret for himself her attitude and expression. Some think
that because she turns her face away she is shrinking from her son in ter-
ror. Yet her expression is so gentle that others say she is nestling close to
him for protection. This is certainly as we should imagine the situation.
When she was a young mother, she was proud to take care of her child.
And now on this great day she is equally proud to let him take care of her.
As he clung to her, his mother, so she now clings to him, the Judge.

Looking at the composition of the picture, we see that her figure com-
pletes a pyramid, whose apex [90] is the uplifted hand of the Judge, and
whose base lies along the cloud supporting his feet and hers. This gives
proper stability to the figures which dominate the whole great picture.
Considered in a larger way, the pyramid is itself the upper part of a long
oval which keeps the central group apart from the surrounding host.

The picture of the Last Judgment was painted by Michelangelo on the
end wall of the Sistine Chapel, over the altar, nearly twenty years after the
completion of the ceiling frescoes. There is a great difference between the
two works. The figures on the ceiling are strong and powerful, their attitudes spirited and graceful. Those in the Last Judgment are huge and cum-
bersome, their attitudes strained and violent. The entire effect of the vast
company of colossal figures is awe-inspiring, but not pleasing.

It is a relief to fix our eyes upon the central portion. Here the painter expressed an idea at once noble and original. The figure of the Christ has not
the delicate beauty of the dead Christ in the Pietà or the finished elegance of
the Christ Triumphant, but he has the splendid vigor of a forceful character. The Mother, less grand and noble than in the bereavement of the
Pietà, less proud than in her young motherhood, is a gentle and lovely creature. Thus the intensely masculine is completed by the delicately feminine,
and the artist shows us ideal types of manhood and womanhood.

[91]

XVI

PORTRAIT

In the pictures of this collection we have learned something of the work of Michelangelo as a sculptor and a painter. He was an artist whose personality was so strongly impressed upon his work that we have come thus to know, to a certain extent, the man himself. His, as we have seen, was not a happy nature, and many of the circumstances of his life conspired against his happiness.

In his early youth he seemed strangely aware of his own superior gifts and was often so overbearing that he made enemies. The story is told of a quarrel he had with a young man named Torrigiano, in whose company he was copying some frescoes in a church in Florence. Stung by some tormenting words of Michelangelo, Torrigiano retaliated with a blow of the fist, which crushed his companion's nose, and disfigured him for life.

Michelangelo's real education began in the palace of Lorenzo the Magnificent, who discovered the lad's talent and made him a favorite. "He sat at the same table with Ficino, Pico, and Poliziano, listening to dialogues on Plato, and drinking in the golden poetry of Greece. Greek literature and philosophy, expounded by the men who had discov [92] ered them, first moulded his mind to those lofty thoughts which it became the task of his life to express in form. At the same time he heard the preaching of Savonarola. In the Duomo and the cloister of S. Marco another portion of his soul was touched, and he acquired that deep religious tone which gives its majesty and terror to the Sistine." [37] In the gardens of S. Marco he had Lorenzo's fine collection of antiquities to study, and learned from them the secrets of Greek sculpture.

[37] Symonds, in Renaissance in Italy: The Fine Arts.

In all these opportunities it would seem that Michelangelo was a most fortunate person. Nor did he lack proper appreciation; the Pietàplaced him at once on a pinnacle of fame, and the David was heartily admired.

It was when he entered the service of the Pope that his troubles began. He was never thereafter a free man. His genius was at the disposition of a series of men, each ambitious for his own fame, and caring little for the artist's personal aspirations. His proud nature was bitterly humiliated by this sacrifice of his independence. Sometimes he openly rebelled, but in the end was always obliged to yield to papal authority.

Michelangelo's sternly upright spirit found also much to sadden him in the corruption of the times. He was a lover of righteousness as well as a lover of liberty, and he greatly mourned the evils which surrounded him.

One of the pleasantest traits in his character was [93] his warm affection for the members of his family and for the few whom he honored with his friendship. One of the latter was Vittoria Colonna, a woman of strong and beautiful character, who brought much brightness into his life.

Our portrait shows him somewhat past middle life when occupied with many important concerns. We can read in the face something of the character of the man. It is certainly not a handsome face, for any good looks he might once have boasted were destroyed by his broken nose. It is nevertheless a face full of rugged strength, with not a little kindliness in the expression. Here is a man whose enmity we should avoid, but whose friendship we should value above rubies.

It is the face of a lonely man. Michelangelo had to suffer the loneliness of genius. No one could fully understand him. He stood apart, towering like a giant above his fellow men.

On the four hundredth anniversary of Michelangelo's birthday, some verses were written by an American poet, Christopher Cranch, which one should read while looking at this portrait: —

> "This is the rugged face
> Of him who won a place
> Above all kings and lords;
> Whose various skill and power
> Left Italy a dower
> No numbers can compute, no tongue translate in words.

> "Patient to train and school
> His genius to the rule
> Art's sternest laws required;
> [94] Yet, by no custom chained,
> His daring hand disdained

The academic forms by tamer souls admired.

"In his interior light
Awoke those shapes of might
Once known that never die;
Forms of titanic birth,
The elder brood of earth,
That fill the mind more grandly than they charm the eye.

"Yet when the master chose,
Ideal graces rose
Like flowers on gnarled boughs;
For he was nursed and fed
At beauty's fountain head
And to the goddess pledged his earliest warmest vows."

The poet describes still further the artist's character, and then enumerates some of his great works. Whatever occupied him —

"Still proudly poised, he stepped
The way his vision swept,
And scorned the narrower view.
He touched with glory all
That pope or cardinal,
With lower aim than his, allotted him to do.

"So stood this Angelo
Four hundred years ago;
So grandly still he stands,
Mid lesser worlds of art,
Colossal and apart,
Like Memnon breathing songs across the desert sands."

[95]

PRONOUNCING VOCABULARY OF PROPER NAMES AND FOREIGN WORDS

The Diacritical Marks given are those found in the latest edition of Webster's International Dictionary.

EXPLANATION OF DIACRITICAL MARKS.

A Dash (¯) above the vowel denotes the long sound, as in fāte, ēve, tīme, nōte, ūse.

A Dash and a Dot (-˙) above the vowel denote the same sound, less prolonged.

A Curve (ˇ) above the vowel denotes the short sound, as in ădd, ĕnd, ĭll, ŏdd, ŭp.

A Dot (˙) above the vowel a denotes the obscure sound of a in past, abāte, Amĕrica.

A Double Dot (¨) above the vowel a denotes the broad sound of a in fᵃther, ᵃs.

A Double Dot (..) below the vowel a denotes the sound of a in ball.

A Wave (~) above the vowel e denotes the sound of e in hẽr.

A Circumflex Accent (^) above the vowel o denotes the sound of o in b·· ·

c sounds like s.

c sounds like k.

s sounds like z.

g is hard as in gēt.

g is soft as in gĕm.

Adōnĭs.
Æneas (ē´nē̆ăs); Æneid (ē´nē̆ĭd).
Ămazŏn.
Ămbrōse.
Ănathŏth.
Anchises (ăn kīsēz).
Ănnō Dŏmĭnī.
Apŏllō.
Ăppĭan.
Ărĭmathēa.

Babylon (băbĭ lŭn); Băbylōnĭan.

Beethoven (bātō vŭn).

Bĕlshăzzar.

Bĕthlēhĕm.

Bĕth-pē·· br> Bramante (br䌰tā).

Bugiardini (b $\overline{oo}$ jär dēnē).

Buonarroti (b $\overline{oo}$ ō när rŏtē).

Canaan (kānan or kānā·an).

Celano (chā·l䌰ō).

Cencio, Bernardo (bẽr när dō· chĕnchē ō).

Chaldean (kăl dēan).

Colonna, Vittoria (vēt tōrē䌰ō lŏnn䌰

Condivi (kōn dēvē).

Cosimo (kōzē mō).

Cristo Risorto (krēstō· rē z·· ō).

Cum 㧌kūmē).

Cyrus (sīrŭs).

Daniel (dănyĕl or dănĭ ĕl).

Dăntē.

Daphne (dăfnē).

Darĭŭs.

Dēlĭan.

Delphi (dĕlfī).

Dēmŏs.

Dies Ir䌰dēās ērī or dīēz īrē).

Dionigi, di San (dē s䌰dē ō· nējē).

Domine, quo vadis (dōmē nā; kwō w䌰īs or dŏmī nē, kwō vādĭs).

Doni, Angelo (䌰jā lō dōnē).

Douay (d $\overline{oo}$ ā).

Duomo (d $\overline{oo}$ ōmō).

Erŏs.

Febbre, della (dĕll䌰ĕbbrā).

Ficino (fē chē'nō).
[96] Franciscan (frăn sĭs'kan).
Frizzi, Federigo (fā̇ dā̇ rē'gō̇ frēt'sē).

G□ann ·jō̇'v□nē).

Giuliano (j ōō lē □ō).
Gōlī'aͱh
Gotti (gŏt'tē).
Gualfonda (gw□ŏn'd□

Hĕl'lĕspŏnt.
Huguenot (hū'gēnŏt).

Infĕr'nō.
Isaiah (ī zā'ya).
Israel (ĭz'rā̇ ĕl).

Jameson (jā'mĕ sŭn).
Jēho·kĭm.
Jĕrēmī'ah.
Jerome (jē rōm' or jĕr'ŏm).
Jĕrū'salĕm.
Jē'thrō.
Jōsī'ah.
Jud□ (jū dē'a).
Jū'dah.
Jū'pĭtĕr.

Kugler (k ōō g'lĕr).

Lăz'arŭs.
Lēăn'dĕr.
Lŏm'bardṣ

Măg'dālēne.
Mē'dĭan.
Medici (mā'dē chē).
Mĕm'nŏn.

Mē'nē.
Michelangelo (mē kĕl 鵒jā˙lō).
Mĭd'ĭaṅ,
Milan (mĭl'aṅ or mĭ lăn').
Milanesi (mē l騰ā'zē).
Mō'ăb.
Morpheus (m · · ūs).

Năz'aṙĕth.
Nē'bō.
Nebuchadnezzar (nĕb ū kăd nĕz'zăr).
Nemour (nĕ m o͞o r').
Nē'rō.

Oliphant (ŏl'ĭ faṅt).

Palazzo Vecchio (p鼦膝sō˙vĕk'kē ō).
Păl'ĕstīne.
Pater Patri枕p雄ār p雄rē ī or pā'tẽr pā'trĭ ē).
Pausanias (pa̤ā'nĭ ăs).
Pensiero, Il (ēl pĕn sē ā'rō);
Pensieroso (pĕn sē ā˙rō'zō).
Pharaoh (fā'rō).
Phĭlĭs'tĭne.
Piazza della Signoria (pē 膝s躍ĕl'l躬en yō˙rē'鰺
Pico (pē'kō).
Piet · pē ā˙t厥.
Pietro in Vincoli (pē ā'trō˙ēn vēn'kō˙lē).
Pitti, Bartolommeo (b鰭tō˙lŏm mā'ō˙pĕt'tē).
Plā'tō.
Poliziano (pō˙lēt sē 隱ō)
py̆th'ĭ aː

Raphael (r陽ā ĕl).

Rucellai (r o͞o chĕl l陽#275;).

Săc'rĭsty̆.
Santarelli (s騸t躬ĕl'lē).

Savonarola (s躱ō˙n躰ō'l鞣

Scappuci, Mario (m榷ē ō˙sk魑p $\overline{OO}$ *'chē).*
Sĕs'tŏs.
Sĭb'yl.
Sĭm'ēŏn.
Sistine (sĭs'tēn).
Solari, Cristoforo (krēs tŏf'ō˙rō˙sō'l榷ē).
Stabat Mater (stā'băt mā'tẽr or st隘麇m榷ār).
Strozzi, Giovan Battista (jō˙v鶞 b麇tēs't舳trŏt'sē).
Sty̆x.
Swĭn'bŭrne.
Sy̆m'ŏnḏs.

Tarquin (t塢kwĭn).
tē'kĕl.
terribilit ⋅ tĕr rē bē lē t瞰.
Torrigiano (t ⋅ ⋅ ē j隱ō).

Uffizi ($\overline{OO}$ *f fēt'sē).*
Upharsin (ū˙f塢sĭn).

Urbano, Pietro (pē ā'trō˙ $\overline{OO}$ *r b隱ō).*

Urbino ($\overline{OO}$ *r bē'no).*

Varj dei Porcari, Metello (mā˙tĕl'lō˙v榷ē dā' ē p ⋅ ⋅ 榷ē).
Vasari (v舳榷ē).
Vatican (văt'ĭ kȧn).
Virgil (vẽr'jĭl).
Vŭl'gāte.

Zĕdēkī'ah.
Zephaniah (zĕf a˙nī'a).

[97]

AUTHORS' PORTRAITS

FOR SCHOOL USE

Sample of the portraits in "Masterpieces of American Literature" and "Masterpieces of British Literature," described on the second page of this circular.

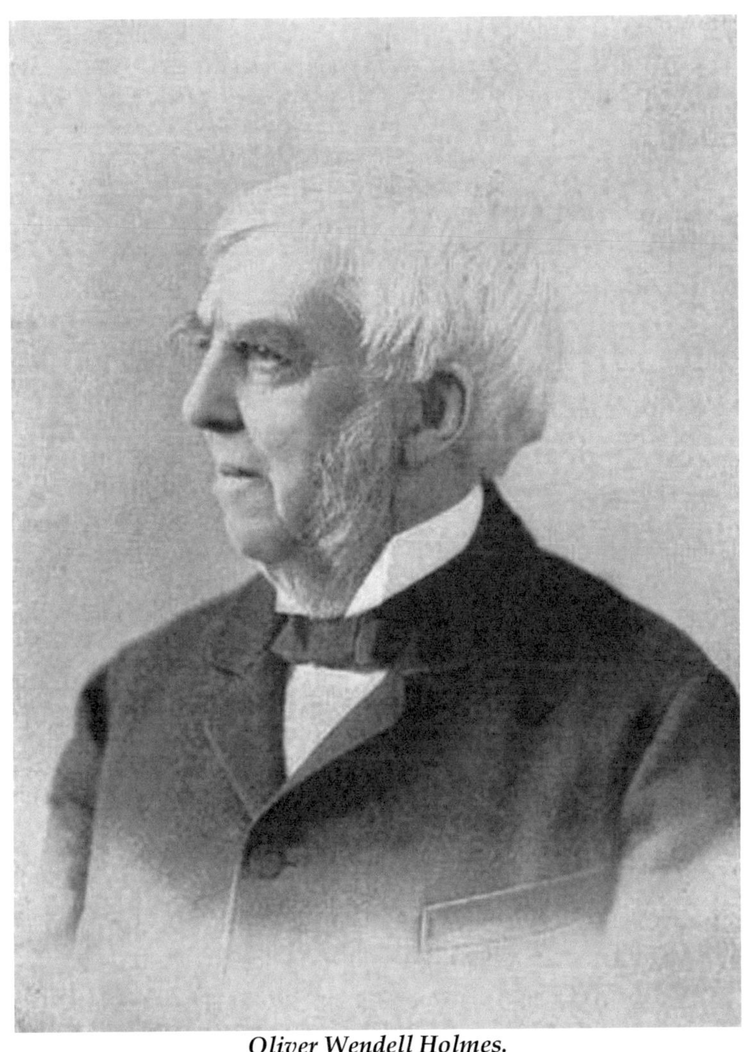

Oliver Wendell Holmes.

PORTRAITS OF AUTHORS

AND PICTURES OF THEIR HOMES

FOR THE USE OF PUPILS IN THE STUDY OF LITERATURE

We have received so many calls for portraits of authors and pictures of their homes suitable for class and note-book use in the study of reading and literature, that we have decided to issue separately the twenty-nine portraits contained in "Masterpieces of American Literature" and "Masterpieces of British Literature," and the homes of eight American authors as shown in the Appendix to the newly revised edition of "Richardson's Primer of American Literature."

PORTRAITS

AMERICAN.

BRYANT.
EMERSON.
EVERETT.
FRANKLIN.
HAWTHORNE.
HOLMES.
IRVING.
LONGFELLOW.
LOWELL.
O'REILLY.
THOREAU.
WEBSTER.
WHITTIER.

BRITISH.

ADDISON.
BACON.
BROWN.
BURNS.
BYRON.
COLERIDGE.
COWPER.
DICKENS.
GOLDSMITH.
GRAY.
LAMB.
MACAULAY.
MILTON.

RUSKIN.
TENNYSON.
WORDSWORTH.

HOMES OF AUTHORS

BRYANT.
EMERSON.
HAWTHORNE.
HOLMES.
LONGFELLOW.
LOWELL.
STOWE.
WHITTIER.

Sold only in lots of ten or more, assorted as desired.

Ten, assorted, postpaid, 20 cents.

Each additional one in the same package, 1 cent.

In lots of 100 or more, assorted, 1 cent each, postpaid.

For mutual convenience please send a remittance with each order. Postage stamps taken.

HOUGHTON, MIFFLIN & CO.

4 Park Street, Boston; 11 East 17th Street, New York:

378-388 Wabash Avenue, Chicago.

ORNAMENTS

FOR SCHOOL-ROOMS

THE ATLANTIC LIFE-SIZE PORTRAITS

Of Whittier, Lowell, Emerson, Hawthorne, Longfellow, Holmes, Bryant. Size, 24 by 30 inches. Lithographs, $1.00, net, each, postpaid. Teachers' price, 85 cents, net, each, postpaid.

MASTERPIECES PORTRAITS.

For descriptions and prices see other pages of this circular.

HOMES OF AMERICAN AUTHORS.

For descriptions and prices see other pages of this circular.

LONGFELLOW'S RESIDENCE.

A colored lithograph of the historic mansion ("Washington's Headquarters") at Cambridge, in which Mr. Longfellow lived for forty years. Size, 12 by 16 inches. Price, 50 cents, net, postpaid.

FINE STEEL PORTRAITS

(The size of cabinet photographs) of over ninety of the most celebrated American and European Authors. The 25-cent portraits and the 75-cent portraits are printed on paper measuring 9 by 12 inches, and the $1.00 portraits 11 by 14 inches. A list with prices to teachers may be had on application.

HOUGHTON, MIFFLIN & CO.

4 Park Street, Boston; 11 East 17th Street, New York;

378-388 Wabash Avenue, Chicago.

AUTHORS' HOMES, FOR SCHOOL USE.

Sample of the pictures of authors' homes in the newly revised edition of Richardson's Primer of American Literature, described on the second page of this circular.

[Illustration: HOLMES'S BIRTHPLACE The Gambrel Roofed House, Cambridge]

THE RIVERSIDE ART SERIES

In the Riverside Literature Series the reader's attention is fixed on a great work of art in letters, with only such help as will make it more intelligible; in like manner in the Riverside Art Series the picture is the object of study, and the text is its interpretation.

Each book contains pictures which are representative of the work of a famous painter, and the most faithful reproductions of the originals have been secured. Valuable suggestions also are given by the editor as aids for further study. The editor of the Series, Miss Estelle M. Hurll, is well known by her recent valuable edition of the works of Mrs. Jameson, and her Life of Our Lord in Art.

The books of this Series will have a value as texts in art classes, as supplementary readers in schools, as guides to the best pictures in galleries both abroad and in this country, and as handy books of reference to the general reader in regard to matters pertaining to the best art.

Four numbers are assigned for publication each school year in October, December, February, and April.

1899-1900.

1. Raphael.
2. Rembrandt.
3. Michelangelo.
4. Jean Fran篩s Millet.

1900-1901.

5. Sir Joshua Reynolds.
6. Murillo.
7. Greek Sculpture.
8. Titian.

Other numbers in preparation.

Each volume is 12mo in size, of about 100 pages.

Price in paper, 30 cents, net; in cloth, 40 cents, net.

SPECIAL SUBSCRIPTION OFFER.

Any four consecutive numbers, in paper, $1.00, net; in cloth $1.50, net.

HOUGHTON, MIFFLIN AND COMPANY

4 Park St., Boston; 11 East 17th St., New York;

378-388 Wabash Avenue, Chicago.